THE CHRISTIAN ETHIC OF
LOVE

Contemporary Evangelical Perspectives Series

Archaeology and the Bible – Wiseman and Yamauchi
*Biblical Criticism – Historical, Literary
    and Textual* – Harrison/Waltke/Guthrie/Fee
The Blessed Hope and the Tribulation – Walvoord
The Christian Ethic of Love – Geisler
Christianity and the Age of the Earth – Young
Christianity Confronts Culture – Mayers
Christianity in a Revolutionary Age – Latourette
Chronological Aspects of the Life of Christ – Hoehner
A Chronology of the Hebrew Kings – Thiele
The Church and the Tribulation – Gundry
Communicating Christ Cross-Culturally – Hesselgrave
Cultural Anthropology: A Christian Perspective – Grunlan
    and Mayers
Essentials of Wesleyan Theology – Mickey
Evolution: Nature and Scripture in Conflict – Pun
From Sabbath to Lord's Day – Carson
Genetic Engineering: The Ethical Issues – Anderson
The Growth of the Church in Africa – Falk
Herod Antipas – Hoehner
History of the Expansion of Christianity – Latourette
Inspiration and Canonicity of the Bible – Harris
Jesus: Human and Divine – McDonald
John Calvin: His Influence in the Western World – Reid
Luke: Historian and Theologian – Marshall
Man and Woman in Biblical Perspective – Hurley
Mark: Evangelist and Theologian – Martin
The Ministry and Message of Paul – Longenecker
The Old Testament in the New – Johnson
Psychology Gone Awry – Cosgrove
A Shorter Life of Christ – Guthrie
A Survey of Bible Prophecy – Ludwigson
A Theology of Church Growth – Peters
What's Gone Wrong With the Harvest? – Engel/Norton
What You Should Know About Homosexuality – Keysor
The Word of God and the Mind of Man – Nash

THE CHRISTIAN ETHIC OF
LOVE

Norman L.
Geisler

ZONDERVAN
PUBLISHING HOUSE
OF THE ZONDERVAN CORPORATION | GRAND RAPIDS, MICHIGAN 49506

*To two faithful
friends in Christ*
BOB and MARYANN SAMMS

THE CHRISTIAN ETHIC OF LOVE
© 1973 by the Zondervan Corporation

Library of Congress Catalog Card No. 73-8362
ISBN 0-310-24921-X

Unless otherwise noted, Scripture quotations are from
The Revised Standard Version of the Bible, copyright
© 1946 and 1952 by the Division of Christian
Education of the National Council of Churches,
and are used by permission.

Printed in the United States of America

83   84   85   86   87   88 — 10   9

Contents

Chapter 1

Love: the Only Absolute

Are there any absolutes? Is everything relative? For example, what is right for one person is wrong for another. What was wrong at one time is now right. It is wrong to use words like "never" and "always" as applied to right and wrong. These are widespread views. But are they really correct? Let us examine them carefully.

THE IMPOSSIBILITY OF DENYING ABSOLUTES

The ancient Greek philosopher, Heraclitus, said, "No one steps into the same river twice, for fresh waters are ever upon him." All is in flux; nothing appears permanent or abiding. Nothing is changeless except change itself. Later, the sophist, Cratylus, held that no man steps into the same river even once. There is no essence or substance there at all, just movement. When asked if he existed, Cratylus replied by simply wiggling his finger, indicating that he too was in flux.

In the modern world two other areas of study have lent support to the flux philosophy. Anthropologists report that very few if any actions are held to be wrong by all people everywhere. Of the traditional moral taboos, even killing and incest are considered right by some tribes. Scarcely anything held wrong by some group of men is not believed to be right by another people. Add to this cultural relativity the scientific relativity of time and space propounded by Einstein and one can readily understand the almost complete aversion of absolutes in modern thinking.

The popularity of denying that there are any things absolutely right or wrong is evident in the craze for situational ethics. Everything is relative to the situation, we are told. Lying, committing adultery and even killing can all be justified if the circumstances call for them. Nothing is wrong in and of itself for all men at all times and in all such circumstances.

There is a strange inconsistency in this denial of all absolutes and it is this: there is no way to deny absolutes without implying an absolute of one's own in the process of the denial. To illustrate, the person who says that one should never use the word "never" just used it himself. To say that it is always wrong to use the word "always" is to be caught in the trap of using a universal to deny that there are any things universally so. One cannot be absolutely sure there are no absolutes without violating his own contention that there are no absolutes.

I once had a university professor who denied that the Ten Commandments were universally true. "They all have exceptions," he argued. He then proceeded to list his own two commandments which he said could not be found in the Bible, "Be intelligent and be tolerant." When asked if there were any exceptions to these two commandments, he replied: "One should be tolerant to everyone, *except* those who are not tolerant." The student did not further embarrass the professor by asking if he would be intelligent to everyone except those who were not intelligent. The inconsistency was apparent enough. To be consistent the professor would have to agree that there were really no exceptions to his commandments. But how about Moses' ten? Were professor X's two commands absolute and Moses' ten relative? The truth of the matter is that there is no way to avoid absolutes.

Even the so-called progressivism of John Dewey, which appears to deny that there are moral absolutes, has at least one of its own. "Progress" or "achievement" was the norm by which all else was to be judged for Dewey. Something was right if it promoted "progress" and wrong if it did not. And Einstein recognized that all cannot be relative, positing absolute spirit to which everything else was relative. After all, it does not make sense to say this is relative to that and that to the other, etc. unless there is something to which everything else is relative but is not itself relative. Absolute change is no more possible than lifting a world by a stick with a fulcrum in mid-air. Even change is not possible unless there is an unchanging base by which its movements can be measured. When Cratylus destroyed the "river" he used change to destroy change, which brings us right back to the unchanging. Absolutes may not always be desired but they cannot be avoided.

The dilemma of the relativist may be illustrated from Winnie the Pooh. Because of Winnie's notorious appetite, Mr. Rabbit answers Winnie's knock on his door by saying, "Nobody home." To this Winnie responds, "There must be somebody home or else he could not say, 'Nobody home.'" Winnie is right. Mr. Rabbit cannot deny his own presence, unless he is present to deny it. Likewise, the relativists cannot hold that all is relative unless there is some unchangeable ground on which they can stand to make their affirmation. Otherwise, they are trying to relativize all else without allowing their own position to be relativized.

Aristotle dramatized the difficulty well by asking the skeptics of his day if they existed. If they said "yes," then they were sure of something. If they said "no," they were refuting themselves. For they had to exist in order to say "no." If they said nothing at all, then Aristotle would assume they did not exist and proceed to speak with someone who did exist. In like manner, anyone who opens his mouth to deny moral absolutes is thereby revealing he has one (or more) of his own. And if he has not opened his mouth, then he has not denied anything which the Christian wishes to affirm.

Affirming and Defending Moral Absolutes

But what are these moral absolutes Christians desire to affirm? Are there not many things which claim to be absolute but do in fact permit of exceptions? Are there not non-Christian candidates for the positions of the moral absolute? What about the alleged absolutes which conflict with each other? These problems must be answered, if we are to defend the absolute nature of Christian morality.

Simply to show that the relativist is wrong does not automatically justify the Christian position. Name some moral absolutes, we are challenged.

In his book, *Mere Christianity*, C. S. Lewis names several moral principles which have no exceptions. No people anywhere have ever held that cruelty to children is right nor rape nor betraying one's benefactor. Nor has any civilization ever believed it was right to kill any man they wanted or to take any woman they wanted to at any time. There have always been limits on these relationships. Contrary to popular belief, argues Lewis, moral principles are not vastly different from people to people; they are very similar. * Indeed, some have sought to reduce all of these to one basic moral absolute.

The German philosopher, Immanuel Kant, identified this absolute moral principle as the "categorical imperative." It was the one unconditional duty binding on all men. This duty, said Kant, is discoverable when one asks himself this question: "Could one will that his action (say, lying or murdering) be a universal law for all men?" If not, then it is wrong. Obviously, one could not will lying to be universal for were lying universal there would be no more truth to lie about and then even lying would be impossible. In brief, universal lying would be self-defeating. Likewise, if murder were universal there would be no more people to murder. This too is a dead-end street, so to speak. Therefore, we must conclude that lying and murder are universally wrong.†

The Jewish philosopher, Martin Buber, held that maintaining an "I-thou" relation, not an "I-it"

* See the appendix to Lewis' *Abolition of Man* where he lists and shows the similarity of the great moral codes of the great civilizations.

† The problem of whether one should ever lie to save a life will be discussed in Chapter Eight.

relation, with other persons was a moral absolute. People should be treated as ends in themselves and not as means to an end. One must sustain a person-to-person and not a person-to-thing relationship with other people. Persons are to be loved and things are to be used. We must never use people and love things. The "I-thou" is a universal norm for human behavior which admits of no exceptions.

It does not take too much analysis to discover that the moral principles of Kant and Buber are not dissimilar from the Christian love principle. Jesus summarized the whole law into this: "Whatever you wish that men would do to you, do so to them" (Matt. 7:12). Clearly, murdering, deceiving and using other people is not loving them. Conversely, if one loves others as himself, then he would not do these things to them for he does not wish to be treated this way himself. In effect, there are not many conflicting candidates for the one irreducible moral absolute — one must always love. There are no exceptions. There are some alternatives to love, such as indifference and hate. But these prove to be self-defeating. For even those who practice them object when others treat them in the same manner. Further, if everyone practiced hate and/or indifference, then meaningful human relationship would be completely nullified. Love is the only candidate for moral absoluteness which is not self-defeating.

Further, love is the only candidate which is universally recognized. Notice, we did not say universally practiced. Morality is not determined by what men *do* but by what they *ought* to do. "Ought" is not discovered from "is" by observation of the practices of men. One may believe heartily that he *ought* to love his neighbor but actually fail to *do* so. Hence, to judge the real moral beliefs of men by their actual moral behavior is a mistake. A man's moral behavior reveals only what he does, not necessarily what he thinks ought to be done. Simply because men practice things like incest, murder and immorality does not mean that these are their moral principles. Murderers do not like to be killed, thieves do not desire to be robbed, etc.

If we cannot determine one's moral beliefs from his behavior, then how can it be done? There are two other ways: by what they *say* ought to be done, and by what they *expect* others to do to them. We have already noted that the great creeds and moral statements are very similar and reducible to the absolute of love. Men say that love is the thing men ought to do. Non-Christians no less than Christians hold that love is essential. Bertrand Russell, who is famous for his book *Why I Am Not a Christian*, later wrote, "What the world needs is Christian love or compassion." * Erich Fromm, the noted psychoanalyst, declared that the lack of love is at the root of all psychological problems. Kant's categorical imperative and Buber's I-thou relation are one with the Golden Rule. Even Confucius had the same basic principle, although it was stated negatively, viz., do not do unto others what you do not want them to do unto you. Basically, moralists have *said* the same thing down through the years about what is absolutely right or wrong. Love is right and not loving is wrong. Most of

* See *Human Society in Ethics and Politics*, p. viii.

the differences in viable moral codes reflect varia-
tions in understanding love and how it is to be
applied. The remaining differences are due to
inconsistencies within the various expressions or
between the expressions and the basic expectations of the one expressing them.

The most fundamental test of the morality of
a course of action is rooted in one's own moral
expectations. It is not how one wishes to treat
others but *how he wishes to be treated* by others
which determines what one really believes is right.
More fundamental than either moral actions or
moral expressions are moral expectations. A young
man, for instance, may desire to behave some-
what differently toward a young lady than he
would desire some other young man to behave
with his daughter. What we really expect of
others toward us and ours is the key to our real
moral beliefs. As Jesus said, "Whatever *you wish
that men would do to you*" is the basis for what
you ought to do to them. Each man is to be
judged out of his own mouth (expressions) and
by his own heart (expectations). For by his
mouth he says what should be done and in his
own heart he knows what he expects others to do
to him.

Thus the question of whether love is the moral
absolute is discoverable in human experience in
several ways. First, do observations of human
lives indicate that all men expect to be loved?
The evidence is overwhelming for an affirmative
answer. Secondly, each man by introspection can
ask, "Do I expect others to treat me with love?"
Any who would attempt to deny the obvious answer belie by their behavior their real desire to
be loved. It seems safe to conclude that all men

expect to be loved and therefore ought to love others.

Not to love others is either to deny they are persons or to be inconsistent with one's own moral expectations. If one expects to be loved, then he ought to love other persons. To deny them love is to deny their personhood. For an understanding of one's own expectations reveals that *as a person* he expects love. And if a person *as such* calls for love, then love cannot be consistently limited only to some persons or to one person (viz., one's self). If one discovers in himself that a person demands love, then that love demands that he apply it to other persons as well. The evasive question, "Who are persons?" can be answered the same way Jesus replied to the lawyer who said, "Who is my neighbor?" (Luke 10:29). A person is anyone who is in need of love. Go and show love to persons.

Chapter 2

God: the Nature of Absolute Love

We have seen that men need love and express love but they do not constitute love. Love is something men *have*, not something they *are*. Yet love is an absolute; it never changes. The ultimate source of love must be as changeless as love itself. Christians identify this source with God. The Bible says that "God is love" (1 John 4:16). What comes from God is of God. He cannot give love which He does not have to give. What God provides for others He "possesses" within Himself. More correctly, God does not have love; He *is* love. Thus no meaningful love ethic can avoid the knowledge of the God of love revealed in Scripture.

But the command to love means nothing unless one knows what love means. And the meaning of love is found in God. For God is love. Ignorance of the nature of God will mean ignorance of the nature of absolute love. In brief, the Christian love ethic is no more secure than its source and no more applicable to life than our knowledge of that source.

THE SOURCES OF THE KNOWLEDGE OF GOD AS LOVE

There are two basic sources for our knowledge of God: human experience and the Scriptures. Since the latter is more explicit we will concentrate on it. But first, what can be known about God through human experience?

In general, the knowledge of God through human experience informs us that there is a God who cares. As Paul said to the heathen at Lystra, God "did not leave himself without a witness, for he did good and gave you from heaven rains and fruitful seasons, satisfying your hearts with food and gladness" (Acts 14:17). The Psalmist said of God, "Thou openest thy hand, thou satisfiest the desire of every living thing" (145:16). Noah had been promised by God, "While the earth remains, seedtime and harvest, cold and heat, summer and winter, day and night, shall not cease" (Gen. 8:22). Nature is a witness to God's love in keeping this promise. Paul reminded the non-Christian philosophers on Mars Hill that God "gives to all men life and breath and everything" (Acts 17:25). There is a witness in nature to all men that there is a God who made them and who cares for their needs (cf. Rom. 1:19, 20).

Our knowledge of God's love is not limited to what is usually called Nature. God has revealed His love to men through the love of other human beings. "Love is of God, and he who loves is born of God," John declared (1 John 4:7). Men are the instruments of God's love (2 Cor. 5:14, 20). Love is from God and those who experience true love are thereby sensing that there is a God who cares.

The most explicit knowledge of God's love,

however, is derived from the Holy Scriptures. From both Testaments and in literally hundreds of places we are told of God's love. Some entire chapters are devoted to love (1 Cor. 13). It is a dominant theme of many books (i.e. Hosea, John), and it is said to be the overall theme of all Scripture (Matt. 5:17; 7:12).

The Nature of God as Love

Even within the Ten Commandments God speaks of "showing steadfast love to thousands of those who love him and keep his commandments" (Exod. 20:6). The psalmist repeats the refrain over and over, "his steadfast love endures for ever" (cf. Ps. 136:1f.). Also repeated throughout the Old Testament is the nature of God revealed to Moses, "A God merciful and gracious, slow to anger, and abounding in steadfast love and faithfulness, keeping steadfast love for thousands, forgiving iniquity and transgression and sin" (Exod. 34:7). And as the experience of Jonah clearly indicates, this love was not limited to Israel. Jonah confessed God's concern for Nineveh, "I knew that thou art a gracious God and merciful, slow to anger, and abound in steadfast love" (Jonah 4:2). God's love comes to fruition in the New Testament, "For God so loved the world that he gave his only Son . . ." (John 3:16). We are told that "greater love has no man than this, that a man lay down his life for his friends" (John 15:13). And yet "God showed his love for us in that while we were yet sinners Christ died for us" (Rom. 5:8).

But perhaps the most astounding thing about love is not that God expresses it but that He consists of it. "God *is* love." Love is God's very nature. To understand God's nature is to know what love is all about. And conversely, to be ignorant of love is to be in the dark about the essence of God. But what is of prime importance for a love ethic is to understand that one's knowledge of the moral absolute can rise no higher than his knowledge of its source in the absolute nature of God as love.

Love is not easy to define. The apostle Paul spent a whole chapter describing it. "Love is patient and kind; love is not jealous or boastful; it is not arrogant or rude. Love does not insist on its own way; it is not irritable or resentful; it does not rejoice at wrong, but rejoices in the right . . ." (1 Cor. 13:4-7 rsv). The last phrase is particularly helpful in defining love, *Love is desiring (and doing) the good of the other.* As Paul said elsewhere, "Love does no wrong to a neighbor" (Rom. 13:10). God desires the good of every creature, and if we are to express love then we must do the same. Love does not necessarily like everything about everyone but it wills their good whether everything is liked or not. God hates sin so much He cannot even look on it (Hab. 1:13), but He loves sinners so much that He gave the best He had for them, * His only Son.

That God wills only the best for every person is manifest in many ways. First, He created them all in His image and likeness (Gen. 1:27). What He is He made all men resemble. The best of His

* When the Bible depicts God as saying, "Jacob I loved, but Esau I hated" (Rom. 9:13) it is not referring to any supposed hatred of God for a person but rather His hatred for the wicked deeds of a nation, the Edomites who came from Esau (cf. Mal. 1:2, 3). Compare Revelation 2:6.

nature is reflected in man, the crown of His creation. Secondly, God sustains man in creation by His loving power. Ezra prayed, "Thou hast made heaven . . . the earth and all that is in them; and thou preservest all of them" (Neh. 9:6). God also desires to redeem all men. Christ died for all men (2 Cor. 5:15). As John said, "He is the expiation for our sins, and not for ours only but also for the sins of the whole world" (I John 2:2). And, further, "the Lord is not . . . wishing that any should perish, but that all should reach repentance" (2 Peter 3:9).

Another characteristic of divine love is that it *gives with no demand for return.* Basically there are three types of love: (1) Egoistic love, which seeks to get but not to give; (2) Mutualistic love, which is involved in a give-and-get relationship; (3) Altruistic love, which gives with no demand to get anything in return. Sometimes these are called respectively, erotic, philic, and agapic loves, from the Greek words for each. Let us examine them more closely.

Erotic love, by this definition, is selfish. Its only purpose is to satisfy itself. Agapic love, on the other hand, desires to satisfy others. It is not what one can get but what he can give that is characteristic of divine love. Philic love is found in friendship. It gives with the expectation that it will receive. Not so with agapic love. God loves even when there is no love in return. God's love is in fact unconditional.

God's love is a giving love even if no one receives it. "God so loved the world that He gave . . . " (John 3:16). But Christ "was in the world and the world was made through Him, yet the world knew Him not. He came to His own, and His people received Him not" (John 1:10, 11). Jesus loved Judas even though He knew Judas would betray Him (John 13:1f.). The crowd cried, "Let Him be crucified" (Matt. 27: 22). Jesus responded, "Father, forgive them; for they know not what they do" (Luke 23:34). Great is the faithfulness of God's love. "If we are faithless, he remains faithful — for he cannot deny himself" (2 Tim. 2:13). Nothing can ultimately separate the believer from God's love (Rom. 8:31-39). But here is the rub. Not all men are believers, not all receive God's love. Some refuse to go God's way and on these He pours out His wrath. To many, it is this wrath that seems incongruous with His love, and which we must now seek to understand in view of His love.

THE RELATION OF WRATH TO GOD'S LOVE

How can God be loving and send people to hell? The Bible says Jesus will one day inflict "vengeance upon those who do not know God and upon those who do not obey the gospel of our Lord Jesus. They shall suffer the punishment of eternal destruction and exclusion from the presence of the Lord . . . " (2 Thess. 1:8, 9). To unbelievers Jesus will say, "Depart from me, you cursed, into the eternal fire prepared for the devil and his angels" (Matt. 25:41). For "if anyone's name was not found written in the Book of life, he was thrown into the lake of fire" (Rev. 20:15). This is described as a place of torment from which there is no return (Luke 16:23, 26) where "men will weep and gnash their teeth" (Matt. 8:12). Is not the existence of such a place incompatible with the nature of God as loving?

The biblical answer to this question is that absolute love, far from being incompatible with hell, actually demands its existence. Love cannot demand a response. No one can force true love. If there are men who do not wish to love God, then God in His love will not force them to love Him. He will, of course, do everything within His loving power to get men to love Him. Indeed, this is what the plan of redemption is all about. But if some are finally impenitent, God will not violate their freedom of destiny. As C. S. Lewis noted, there are only two kinds of people in the universe: first, the kind who say to God, "Thy will be done" and second, the kind to whom God will say, "thy will be done." Hell is the place provided by a long-suffering God for those who refuse to go His way. Having tried all to win them, God will ultimately have to say to some, "All right, have it your way."

If God would allow any unbelievers to enter heaven it would be worse than hell for them. How can those who detest prayer and praise to God bear to remain eternally in a place which does this continually? If they felt uncomfortable for only an hour in church doing this, think of the eternal discomfort if they had to do it forever. Or, to put it more strongly, since heaven is a place where men will bow in worship to God, how could it be considered loving for God to force men to go there when they do not will to worship God, but hate Him? It seems more congruent with the nature of divine love not to compel men to love Him against their will. Hence, God is actually merciful to provide for the unbelieving a place where they can "do their own thing." They have made their own choice how they will live, and it would be unloving to deny it them simply because it is not God's way. God will grant them their choice to continue in their own willful way.

This is not to imply that all men in hell *wish* to be there. There is no doubt about the undesirability of their destiny. On the other hand, they have willed to be there, for they will to have it their way instead of God's. And since there are others who will to have it God's way and since their place (heaven) would be worse for the unbelieving, God has provided a place for those who choose to go their own way. However undesirable their choice may be, they have made it and must live with it.

But what if some one in hell should change his mind? Would not a loving God release him? The biblical answer to this is clear: they are in hell only because God knows they will never change their wills. If a thousand more chances would have helped them, God in love would have given these opportunities. But knowing all things in advance, including the fact that the impenitent will never change their minds, God pronounces them unredeemable and says, "It is appointed for men to die once, and after that comes judgment" (Heb. 9:27). Love, even God's love, has failed to win them but it has not failed to manifest itself. Love has given them the chance for the best and has allowed them to be self-determining in choosing less than that best. God is so loving that He will allow the ultimate insult to His love, the rejection of it.

What, then, is wrath? Wrath results from rejected love. As Lewis so aptly observed, the only place in the universe where men will be free from the perturbations of love is hell. This is reminiscent of the prophet, "Ephraim is joined to idols, let him alone" (Hosea 4:17). Hell is where love is no longer effectively working, no longer wooing for it is no longer possible to win anyone there. Wrath is the result of rejected love. It is not that God no longer loves. His radiant love still shines. But it must be remembered that the same sun which melts wax also hardens clay. The difference is not the source of the energy (or love) but in the receptivity of the object of it. Where there is no longer a will to be open to God's love, there is wrath. Anyone who has tried to love someone who does not wish to be loved can sense in part the frustrations of God's love. And anyone who has rejected the love which others have extended to him has experienced a bit of what hell will be like. It is miserable to be loved and not to open one's self to it. So it is that unbelieving men's souls are like a cup under Niagara Falls upside down. "Where is the love of God and the God of love?" they cry. "My life is empty and meaningless." So it is with all who refuse to turn their souls upward and let the Niagara of infinite love fill their lives. God is loving; He is willing the good of every man, if only they would will their own greatest good.

SOME IMPLICATIONS OF GOD'S LOVE

There are several things about the nature of God as love often obscured by the "soft-soap" version peddled in many circles today. First, love involves discipline. "For the Lord disciplines whom he loves, and chastises every son whom he receives" (Heb. 12:6). For "he who spares the rod hates his son, but he who loves him is diligent to discipline him" (Prov. 13:24). Secondly, love can be very forceful. Jesus, the personification of God's love, manifested anger, spoke sharply to the hypocrites (Matt. 23) and physically expelled the merchants from the temple (John 2). Third, love can fail. The proper rendering of 1 Corinthians 13:8 is "love never ends." It does sometimes fail. In one sense hell is a testimony to the "failure" of the love of God. There is another sense, of course, in which God's love never fails in that it always manifests itself and gives the opportunity for salvation. And surely it is more loving to offer needed goods which will be refused than not to offer them at all. At any rate it seems that for God's love, too, it is better to have loved and to have lost than not to have loved at all.

These characteristics of love will be helpful when the Christian seeks to emulate the love of God in his own life. For, as will be seen, the Christian love ethic is not, as Nietzsche charged, a morality of the weak. Love is as strong and absolute as God. Let the weak beware of it!

Chapter 3

Loving on Two Levels

Love is an absolutely binding imperative for the Christian. God is love and those born of God must express His love. "By this all men will know that you are my disciples, if you have love for one another" (John 13:35). And "If any one says, 'I love God,' and hates his brother, he is a liar; for he who does not love his brother whom he has seen, cannot love God whom he has not seen" (1 John 4:20). "Beloved," wrote John, "I am writing you no new commandment, but an old commandment, which you had from the beginning" (1 John 2:7). Love is a moral imperative for the Christian.

THE TWO GREAT COMMANDMENTS

Loving is an unequivocal command for the Christian but it is not uni-leveled. Love must be manifest on two levels, the love for God and love for one's neighbor. When asked about the great commandment of the law Jesus gave two: "You shall love the Lord *your* God with all your heart, and with all your soul, and with all your mind. This is the great and *first* commandment." "And," He continued, "a *second* is like it, You shall love your

26

neighbor as yourself. On these two commandments depend all the law and prophets" (Matt. 22:37-40). Man's entire moral duty is here summarized in the two-directional movement of love. Vertically, one must love God with his whole self. Horizontally, one must love his neighbor as himself.

The two tables of Moses' law are divided by these two directions of love. The first table of the law expresses the vertical love for God: (1) You shall have no other gods before me; (2) You shall not make any graven images; (3) You shall not take the name of the Lord in vain; (4) Remember the sabbath day to keep it holy. The second table of the law expresses one's love for his neighbor: (5) Honor your father and mother; (6) You shall not kill; (7) You shall not commit adultery; (8) You shall not steal; (9) You shall not bear false witness; (10) You shall not covet. The ten commandments merely spell out what the two commandments summarize. If one loves God he will do the first four and to show his love for other men he must do the last six.

What is noteworthy is that one commandment has priority over the other. One is the "*first* and *great* commandment" and the other is "*second*." God is to be loved *with all one's heart*; the neighbor is to be loved only *as one loves himself*. The clear implication here is that God should be loved supremely but man only finitely. God is absolute and ultimate and as such He demands ultimate love. Man is only the finite resemblance of the infinite God and as such should only be loved in a finite manner. Already, then, the imperative to love is divided. There are two basic objects of love and each is to be loved in a different way.

To love God — to will His good — means to acknowledge His ultimate worth-ship. But no man should be the object of worship as God is. That would be idolatry. Hence, to love man — to will his good — means to recognize his value as a creature in God's image and to treat him accordingly.

These two levels of love imply a third below them, the world created for man's use. Man was told to "subdue it." All the animals, plants and minerals are man's tool for living and serving God. Hence, the obligation of love implies at least a three-level scale of values. God, the supreme value, is at the top. Under Him is man, the most valuable creation in the world. And under man is the world of animals, plants and minerals which are pronounced "good" by God (Gen. 1:31), but which are clearly a lesser good. These material things are not to be *loved* supremely as God nor even finitely as man. In fact they are not really ends to be loved; they are things to be *used*. If they are used for man's good and God's glory, then they have fulfilled their purpose. If they are esteemed of more value than man or God, then they are being misused. Love has two basic levels, one for God and the other for man. Things are to be valued as instruments in the service of the proper human and divine objects of love.

Conflict Between the Two Great Commandments

The fact that there are two levels of love poses a problem for the Christian love ethic, viz., what to do when the two levels conflict. Some have attempted to avoid the conflict by routing all love for God through men. Two Scriptures are cited in support of this position. First, Jesus said "Truly, I say to you, as you did it to one of the least of these my brethren, you did it to me" (Matt. 25: 40). John declared that one cannot love God whom he has not seen if he does not love his brother whom he can see (1 John 4:20). Now whatever else these verses imply they do not teach that the *only* way to love God is to love Him through other human beings. They do say two things: first, one cannot truly love God unless he *also* loves others; second, *one way* to love God is through loving other humans. Nowhere do the Scriptures teach that love to God can be expressed *only* through other humans.

Indeed, sometimes the love for God must transcend and take precedence over the love for others. Such was the case when Abraham was willing to give up his son Isaac for God (Gen. 22). Jesus said, "If any one comes to me and does not hate his own father and mother and wife and children and brothers and sisters, yes, and even his own life, he cannot be my disciple" (Luke 14:26). Clearly, the love for God must be so much more than one's love for any other human that his love for them seems as "hate" compared to his love for God. God must be loved *with all one's heart*. This is much more than loving God merely *as one loves himself*. It would be an insult to God to love Him only as much as one loves himself. God is of infinite value; man is of finite value. God must be loved *more* than anyone else, including one's own self. Jesus said, "If any man would come after me, let him deny himself and take up his cross and follow me" (Matt. 16:24).

The two levels of love, then, are not always in harmony. There is often tension between them.

Sometimes loving one's parents comes in conflict with loving God. Children are told, "obey your parents" as an expression of their love (Eph. 6:1), but only "in the Lord." For the command of parents could be contrary to one's love for God. If a parent commanded his child to hate or curse God or to sin against God in some other way, then clearly the child should disobey his parent. One's love for God takes priority in all conflict situations. The love for the parent whom he is disobeying in order to obey God will seem like "hate" in view of this transcending love for God.

This same conflict between the two levels of love is found in other areas. The Bible strongly enjoins the believer to "be subject for the Lord's sake to every human institution, whether it be to the emperor as supreme, or to governors as sent by him . . ." (1 Peter 2:13). Paul adds, "Let every person be subject to the governing authorities" and "he who resists the authorities resists what God has appointed . . ." (Rom. 13:1, 2). That this submission clearly implied obedience is shown by the fact that the words "submit" and "obey" are used interchangeably of one's relation to government and of other human relationships (cf. 1 Peter 3:1). The apostle wrote to Titus, "Remind them to be submissive to rulers and authorities, to be obedient . . ." (3:1). This commanded obedience notwithstanding, there were times when the apostles found it necessary to disobey the authorities and declare, "We must obey God rather than men" (Acts 5:20).

Indeed, many Old Testament believers before the apostles disobeyed human government with God's approval. The Hebrew midwives refused the king's command to kill all the male children

(Exod. 1:15f.). Daniel disobeyed Darius' ban on private prayer (Dan. 6) and his three Hebrew companions defied Nebuchadnezzar's command to worship a golden image (Dan. 3). In each case their love for God transcended the command to obey human authorities. They loved God more than men and so it ought to be. God is of supreme value; men are less than supreme. Whenever there is a clear conflict between the two, a man must express his love for God, even if it means disobeying such venerable authorities established by God as parents and governors.

Resolving the Conflict
Between the Two Levels of Love

Love is absolute but it is not simple. There are two basic levels of love and they sometimes conflict. One level is of infinite value and the other is finite in value. Our love for each ought to reflect the difference in values.

Normally there is no real conflict between loving God and loving other men. One is a vertical and the other a horizontal relationship. They are in different spheres which usually do not overlap. However, sin confuses the issue. Some men overstep their God-appointed domains and precipitate a conflict for others. For when a parent or a political authority assumes sovereign power and demands ultimate allegiance, then a tension is set up between the two levels of love. It is a forced option and the Christian must choose. And since God is of greater value than man, one's love for God must take precedence over his love for other men.

In terms of the Ten Commandments, it is sometimes necessary to appear to "break" the fifth commandment in order to keep the first commandment. But in actual fact one is not really breaking the lower commandment; rather, he is merely *transcending* it by his obedience to the higher commandment. There is no exception being made to the duty to love on the lower level; but merely an *exemption* in view of one's responsibility to love on the higher level. The lower law of love is not being abolished; it is only being preempted by a higher one. Properly speaking, it is not a transgression but a *suspension* of the lower law of love for the higher law of love. The law of magnetism does not destroy the law of gravity when a magnet picks up a nail; it merely *overpowers* it. Likewise, when the conflicts do arise, then God should be given the preeminence.

Loving God *more* than men does not necessarily mean that one is loving God *instead* of men. It is true that the love for God may necessitate "disobedience" toward men and what may seem by contrast to be a "hate" for them. However, disobedience may be the best way to express one's love for them. Love means to *give* to the sinner, not to give in to his sinful wishes. Love means to *will his good,* not to be willing to go along with his evil. Sometimes the best way to express one's love for someone's good is to resist his evil. A passive resignation to evil is not a true expression of love for someone. Hence, to love God more than others is to love the others more. It is to give God His due by giving to men what is due them, viz., a negative response to a harmful request.

No sane parent gives his child everything he wants. Love provides what the child needs, not everything he wants. The parent wills the best for his child's own good. In like manner, because a man loves God more than anyone else, he will sometimes have to do seemingly hateful things in order to really love that person. Loving God most helps us to love others best.

In brief, the two levels of love are in conflict but never in contradiction. Lower laws of love must sometimes be subordinated to higher ones but are never completely disconnected from them. The highest expression of concern for another human being is to will for them what God commands for them. And God commands them what He requires of all men, viz., that they take their place under God and not take the place of God.

Chapter 4

Loving Others and One's Self

The imperative for the Christian is "love your neighbor as yourself." There are several implications hidden in this command which demand attention. One implication is that the love command implies a love of one's self. The other is that love should be comprehensive and complete. It should cover all men and the whole man, not just his "soul."

LOVING OTHERS COMPREHENSIVELY

Jesus made it clear that the command to love one's "neighbor" was not to be limited to a specific class of people. The grammatical form is singular but the moral intent is plural. God is interested in one's neighbors. The lawyer asked Jesus "who is my neighbor?" Jesus replied with the story of the Good Samaritan who was neighborly (i.e., loving) to a man in need whom he found along the road. Included in the teaching of the story is the point that neighbors are not constituted by certain classes or even geographical locations of people; neighbors are people in need whoever they are and wherever they may be. Neighbors are, in a sense, all men everywhere, for all men are in need of love.

The truth that all men should be loved is not exclusive to the New Testament. The Jewish believers were informed of God's love for all men. God chose their Father Abraham so that through him "All the families of the earth will be blessed" (Gen. 12:3). Moses who first wrote, "you shall love your neighbor as yourself" (Lev. 19:18), also commanded Israel to show concern for the stranger (19:9) and consideration for their enemy (Deut. 20:10f.). Jonah discovered that God loved even the wicked Assyrians (Jonah 4:2). In the New Testament, God's love is offered to all men. The Good News of salvation is for "all nations" (Matt. 28:19). Christ died for the whole world (John 3:16). Christians are commanded to "do good to all men, especially those who are of the household of faith" (Gal. 6:10).

The international implications of God's love notwithstanding, by Jesus' day there were some who had found a "loop-hole" in the love command. It said only to love one's *neighbor,* they reasoned. That would imply that those who were not one's neighbor by proximity were not included. In fact if one was not to love his non-neighbors, then surely he was thereby to be free to hate his enemies. It was this erroneous thinking that Jesus attacked in Matthew 5. "You have heard that it was said, 'You shall love your neighbor and hate your enemy.' But I say to you, Love your enemies and pray for those who persecute you . . ." (vv. 43, 44). Our Lord left no "loop-hole" in the love command. He corrected their misinterpretation of the love command and reinstated again the true intent of the Old Testament.

Love is not to be limited to one's friends or countrymen. Love is comprehensive. All men must be loved for Christ's sake. Everyone is a "neighbor" in the broadest sense of that word. But in a more particular sense the "neighbor" is the person "at hand," the one whose need is near. This is extremely important to the Christian love ethic. For it is evident to the thoughtful that one cannot literally love all men. Even if someone were to try, his love would be spread so thinly over so many that it would not mean very much to any of them. This problem is solved by the biblical principle of centralized loving which begins with one's own and works out from there to all men.

The Christian's most basic earthly love obligation is to care for himself (Eph. 5:29). Unless he does this he will not be able to help others (a drowning man cannot save someone else). Proper self-love is the basis for loving others. "Love your neighbor as you love yourself," is the command. Paul exhorted the believers to work for themselves and provide their own needs (1 Thess. 4:11f.). But more on this later.

Next to loving one's self, the most immediate love responsibility is to one's own family. From the very beginning God made it clear that we are our brother's keepers (Gen. 4:9). No man is a self-sustaining island. He needs the help of others. And each man is obligated to provide for those closest to him. Paul wrote plainly on this point, "If any one does not provide for his relatives, and especially for his own family, he has disowned the faith and is worse than an unbeliever" (1 Tim. 5:8). Parents are to begin in their love by caring for their own children. From this sphere of love they are to move out to their other relatives in need (v. 16). According to the Bible, the next sphere of responsibility is to one's fellow believers in need. "So then," urged Paul, "as we have opportunity let us do good to all men, *especially to those who are of the household of faith*" (Gal. 6: 10). John added, "If any one has the world's goods and sees his brother in need, yet closes his heart against him, how does God's love abide in him?" (1 John 3:17). From the believers the circle is to broaden to include "all men," as much as is possible.

Like a pebble cast into the water, the main thrust of love will be at the center of its responsibility, i.e., to those nearest. But the waves must move out as far as possible. Love is not unlike its kindred virtue, peace. The Christian is taught to love all men "as much as is possible" (cf. Rom. 12:18). And the best way to love all men is to start loving those men closest home. Love is contagious; it will spread once it gets a good start. The best way to set ablaze a whole house is to get a good hot fire going in one central place, not to spread that same heat energy thinly over the whole house. In like manner, the best way to set the world on fire with love is to get it going well in the center of one's relationship with those closest to him. They will be able to pass it on from there.

There are some important implications in this concept of centralized loving, besides the fact that it is the best way to make love comprehensive. First, when there is a conflict as to whom should be loved how much, then those closest to the center of one's love responsibility take priority over those farther out. The hungry neighbor children should not be given the family food needed to nourish his own children. A father has no obligation to buy clothes for the ill-clad of India if his own children will go naked. A mother should take her own child from a burning building first before helping to rescue the neighbor's children. *

Of course, if there is more than enough food and clothes, etc. for one's own, then they should be used for others as well. But adequate love should be expressed at home first before one spreads it elsewhere. Those outside the immediate circle must get the overflow but not the necessities for one's own family. Love's obligation begins at home and then should spread from there as far as it is possible. In this way the ripples from the many centers of love will reach out to the otherwise unloved ones outside these centers.

This same principle of centralized love responsibility is evident both in the life of Christ and in His last word to the disciples. Jesus spent most of His time teaching a small group of men, although He did not neglect the crowd. His whole ministry was located in the homeland and largely to His own people, but a Syrophenician or a Samaritan was included on occasions. The Greeks inquired about a ministry of Jesus for their people, but were informed that Jesus' mission to Jerusalem was more important at that point. The Gospel would spread to Greece later (John 12:20f). Indeed, even after Jesus died and rose He said the Gospel should begin first at home and then go

---

* The question as to which should be rescued first, one's own father or the inventor of a cancer cure is more complex. This writer feels the obligation is to one's own father, since that is the closest relationship to him in the duty at hand to help someone. Guessing long-range results is an uncertain game. One's duty is now, not to divine the future. God will take care of the long-range results if we do our immediate duty.

out from there to all the world. "But you shall
receive power when the Holy Spirit has come
upon you; and you shall be my witnesses in Jerusalem and in all Judea and Samaria and to the
end of the earth" (Acts 1:8). The love for all
comes best when the love for those one is next
to comes first.

LOVING OTHERS COMPLETELY

Love should not only be comprehensive but it
should be complete. The love ethic demands that
we love all men and that we love the whole man,
not just his soul. Lovers of "souls" have a faulty
view of man. They are apparently unaware of
the biblical teaching that man is a unity of soul
and body. The wholeness of man is many faceted
but is essentially one. The dualistic view of man
with a spiritual part called "soul" and a less important part called "body" may come to us from
the Middle Ages. It is not Christian in origin
but Platonic. God made man one in essence even
as God is one in nature (Deut. 6:4). Man is in
God's image and likeness. There is in each of us
only one person and our body is an integral part
of that personhood. The doctrine of the resurrection does not make good sense if a man is complete without his body. Disembodied souls survive
death (Rev. 6:9) but they are in need of embodiment to be fully human in their functions
(2 Cor. 5:1-6).

And since man is a soul-body unity, it is not
strange that the commands of love should be
concerned about this whole man in all of his di-
mensions. Jesus realized the need to give men
food for their physical hunger as He spoke to them
of the "bread of life" (John 6:11f.). Men are

not likely to be impressed by a so-called spiritual love which is unconcerned about their physical and social privations. John made this unmistakably clear when he wrote, "If any one has this world's goods and sees his brother in need, yet closes his heart against him, how does God's love abide in him?" (1 John 4:17). James was no less emphatic in his book: "If a brother or sister is ill-clad and in lack of daily food, and one of you says to them, 'Go in peace, be warmed and filled,' without giving them the things needed for the body, what does it profit? So faith by itself, if it has no works, is dead" (4:15).

The Christian responsibility to love the whole man goes beyond the mere needs of food and clothes, even though these are basic (cf. Lev. 25:35). Men have other social needs as well. There are the lonely and imprisoned who need visiting (Matt. 25:26; James 1:27). The sick need to be healed (James 5:14). There are slaves to be freed. "Let my people go," cried Moses to the oppressive Pharaoh. Oppression of all kinds is forbidden by God. "You shall not wrong a stranger or oppress him. . . . You shall not afflict any widow or orphan" (Exod. 22:21). It is the responsibility of Christian love to oppose oppression, to work for the social relief of all men. Love is concerned about the whole man with all of his needs.

Loving One's Self Correctly

The Christian love ethic implies a proper love for one's self. To love one's neighbor *as himself* one must know how to love himself. Christians have sometimes backed away from self-love because of the stress laid on self-denial in Scripture. Jesus said, "He who loves his life loses it . . ."

(John 12:25). Again, "If any one comes after me and does not hate . . . even his own life, he cannot be my disciple" (Luke 14:26). Paul warned Timothy against men who are "lovers of self" (2 Tim. 3:2). Add to this the confession of the apostle about human depravity — "I know that nothing good dwells within me" — and it might be difficult to see self-love as part of the Christian love ethic.

Actually these Biblical condemnations are not in opposition to loving one's self but against over-loving one's self. A man is to deny the selfishness in himself but not the self from which it comes. It is the sin in one's self which should be hated, not the sinner. Far from condemning self-love the Bible commends it. Paul wrote, "Husbands should love their wives as their own bodies. He who loves his wife loves himself. For no man ever hates his own flesh, but nourishes and cherishes it . . . " (Eph. 5:28, 29). This is scarcely a criticism of proper self-love. A man cares for himself and he ought to do so. He also cares for his wife and he ought to do so. In fact, if he does not know how to care for himself, then how will he know how to care for someone else? When Jesus said to love one's neighbor *as one's self* He clearly implied that one should love himself and that this should serve as the basis for loving others. Human experience has confirmed that those who do not have a proper respect and concern for themselves will be lacking in these same things toward others.

It is not self-love which is wrong; it is the reason some people love themselves which is wrong. To love one's self simply for the sake of loving one's self can be sinful. But to love one's self for the sake of loving others is definitely good. The pilot who provides sleep and denies alcohol for his body loves himself for the sake of his passengers. The pregnant mother who eats proper foods and nutrients loves her body for the sake of her baby, and so on. Providing things for one's self as a creature of God is good; loving one's self as though one were the Creator is a most basic evil (Rom. 1:25). In brief, a Christian should love himself for three reasons: first, because he is made in God's image which is worthy of love whether it is in someone else or one's self; second, because self-love is the basis for loving others; third, because God loves us, and if we do not love ourselves then we do not love what God loves.

In summation, the love imperative includes a comprehensive loving of everyone, beginning with one's self, his own family, and extending to the whole world. Further, love must be complete; it must be a love of the whole man with all of his needs whether they be spiritual, physical, social, or whatever. Love is of God but it is for man — the whole man and the whole of mankind. If all men submitted to God there would be little conflict between the two levels of love. The failure to render to God the things that are His and to others the things that are theirs is the root of much of the conflict between the two levels of love. God neither designed nor desires that the two levels conflict. And despite the conflicts occasioned by man's conditions in this world, God enables the believer to love Himself supremely and others truly, even when it is necessary to displease or disobey other men completely.

Chapter 5

Laws: Putting Love Into Words

There is a rather widespread misbelief that love and law are incompatible. "The law was given through Moses; grace and truth came through Jesus Christ" (John 1:17), is often quoted in support of this view. Or, "you are not under law but under grace" (Rom. 6:14). Now, while it is certainly true that Christians are not under either the ceremonies (Heb. 8-10) or the curses of the Mosaic law (Gal. 3:13), it is also true that the ethical principles embodied in the Mosaic code are binding on the Christian. Further, the eternal ethical principles expressed in the Ten Commandments are not incompatible with the nature of God as love; they are in fact an expression of that love.

LOVE IN THE LAW OF MOSES

The Christian is sometimes faced with a false dilemma; it is either the love of law or the law of love, we are told. Either one is concerned with the love of duty or the duty of love. This makes better poetry than morality. The two are not opposites. "Oh, how I love thy law!" the psalmist exclaimed (119:97). Again, "I love thy commandments above gold, above fine gold" (v. 127). There is nothing wrong with loving the law of God, for God is love and to love His law is to love the expression of His love in the law.

Love is the very basis of the Mosaic law. The opening words of the decalogue are an expression of God's love for His people, "I am the Lord your God, who brought you out of the land of Egypt, out of the house of bondage" (Exod. 20:2). Redemptive grace is foundational to the Ten Commandments which follow. The second commandment repeats the emphasis on love, "I the Lord your God . . . showing steadfast love to thousands of those who love me and keep my commandments" (20:6). Words expressing God's love, such as "mercy," "kindness," "goodness," "favor," "pity," etc. occur oftimes in the Old Testament. "I am the Lord your God, who brought you out of the land of Egypt, out of the house of bondage" — is one of the most repeated truths in the Old Testament. It is repeated in some form some one hundred times or more in the Old Testament. Whoever originated the error that love is exclusively a New Testament teaching was not reading the Old Testament.

Not only did God express His love for Israel as the foundation of the law but the very law itself is an expression of His love. The fifth commandment provides a hint to the intent of all the commandments: do this *that your days may be long* in the land which the Lord your God gives you" (Exod. 20:12). Often attached to other laws we read something like the following: do this *"that the Lord your God may bless you* in all the work of your hands that you do" (Deut. 14:29; 16:15 etc.). In Moses' great farewell speeches he exhorted Israel, "Be careful to do the words of this covenant, *that you may prosper* in all that you do" (Deut. 29:9). From Mt. Gerizim the law was read to the people reminding them, *"And all these blessings shall come upon you* and overtake you, if you obey the voice of the Lord your God. *Blessed* shall you be in the city, and *blessed* shall you be in the field. *Blessed* shall be the fruit of your body . . . *Blessed* shall be your basket . . . *Blessed* shall you be when you come in, and *blessed* shall you be when you go out" (Deut. 28:2-6). The purpose of the law was to bless the people. God loved them and wanted to guide them by His loving laws into a blessed and prosperous life. The cursings are only warnings for those who do not keep the law. And surely warning about the consequences of sin is the loving thing to do.

The giving of the law was an expression of God's love. It was God's way of saying, "I love you so much that I want to give you the guiding principles for the fullest most satisfying life possible." The first table of the law said in essence, "Love God with all your heart. Do not insult His love by serving or worshipping other gods or cursing His name. Show your love by giving one day in seven in special worship of Him." The second table essentially said this: "To have a really blessed life in your interpersonal relations love others as you love yourself. Begin this love at home by respect for your parents. Make sure you also have respect for human life, your neighbor's wife and property. Lying about others or desiring their possessions will not make you happy either." In brief, keeping each law is an expression of one's love. It is spelling out just what the loving course of action is with respect to God and

other men. The laws are just so many ways of
stating what the loving action really is. Law is
stating love in words.

Jesus declared, "Think not that I have come to
abolish the law and the prophets; I have come
not to abolish them but to fulfill them" (Matt.
5:17). And when He affirmed, "But I say unto
you" in contrast to "you have heard that it was
said to the men of old" he was not contrasting
His teaching with that of the Old Testament.
More than ninety times Jesus and the New Testament writers affirm "it is written," citing the Old
Testament as the authority for their teaching (cf.
Matt. 4:4, 7, 10). What was *"said"* by the mis-
interpreters of the law was really not what was
"written" in the law, despite some verbal similarities. This is particularly obvious in the reference, "You have heard that it was said, 'You shall
love your neighbor and hate your enemy'" (Matt.
5:43). Nowhere in the Old Testament is it written
or implied that one should hate his enemies. The
contrary is clearly taught (Lev. 19:9; Deut. 20:
10; Jonah 4:2). When Jesus said, "Love your enemies," He was reaffirming an Old Testament truth.

As a matter of fact, each one of the Ten Commandments is repeated in the New Testament.
Nine of them are repeated almost verbatim. Paul
gives four of them in one place, "The commandments, 'You shall not commit adultery, You shall
not kill, You shall not steal, You shall not covet'
and any other commandment, are summed up in
this sentence, 'You shall love your neighbor as
yourself'" (Rom. 13:8, 9). "Honor your father
and mother" is quoted in Ephesians (6:2). Idol-

atry is condemned in many places (Gal. 5:20;
1 John 5:21), as is lying (Eph. 4:25). Swearing
was condemned by Jesus (Matt. 5:34) and the
supremacy of God is affirmed in several places (cf.
1 Cor. 8:5). This leaves only the commandment
about the sabbath which is preserved in principle
in the Christian Lord's Day, although because
of the resurrection and appearance of the risen
Christ it is now on Sunday instead of Saturday
(Acts 20:7; 1 Cor. 16:2). Thus, one does not avoid
the Ten Commandments by an appeal to the New
Testament law of love; the Ten Commandments
are repeated in the New Testament too. Like the
Old Testament statement of the commandments
they are *summarized* by the love principle but the
latter is not a *substitute* for the former. The New
Testament spells out the commandments too.

If the Ten Commandments are repeated in the
New Testament, then in what sense are New Testament believers "not under law but under grace"?
There is a key passage on this in Galatians chapter
three. "Christ redeemed us from the curse of the
law, having become a curse for us" (v. 13). We
are no longer under the curse of the moral law
of Moses. Christ took the sting of death which
was the result of disobeying the law (1 Cor. 15:
55, 56). But taking away the curse of the law
and abolishing its commands are two different
matters.

Nowhere does the New Testament teach that
the moral principles embodied in the Ten Commandments are not binding upon the Christian.
All of the commandments are restated in the New
Testament, now in the context of grace and not
judgment. It is the same moral law, only the
Mosaic cursings (and even blessings) are not at-

tached to it. For instance, when Paul restates
the blessing attached to the fifth commandment
it is "that you may live long on the earth" (Eph.
6:3), not as Moses said to Israel, "that your days
may be long in the land (of Palestine) which the
Lord your God gives you" (Exod. 20:12). The
commandment is the same but the blessing is different. The commandment about adultery is another example. The Old Testament judgment attached to it was death (Lev. 20:10). There is
no such penalty attached to the New Testament
commandment. The command is the same but the
blessing is different. Removal from the church was a
discipline for adulterers (1 Cor. 5:5f.).

The same is true of other commandments. The
content of the commands is identical from Old
to New Testaments but the *context* is different.
One is a Mosaic context applied to a theocratic
nation; the other is applied to individual believers.
The one had specific sanctions and blessings not
applicable to the other.

Just as the same laws are found in different
countries (say, against speeding) but are really
different laws of different nations, so the eternal
ethical principles embodied in the Mosaic law are
the same ones restated in the New Testament context of grace. It is in this sense that "the law
was given through Moses; grace and truth came
through Jesus Christ." Certainly the Christian is
not under Moses' law any more than an American
who breaks a speeding law in New York is thereby guilty of breaking the law against speeding
in London. Christians are not under Moses' particular codification of the Ten Commandments.
Moses' commandments were stated in a certain
context for a specific people. The Christian lives

in a different "country." When he lies or steals
he is not breaking Moses' law and he does not
pay the consequences of Moses' law. Christians
who lie, steal, etc. are breaking God's eternal law
which was embodied and expressed in the Mosaic
codification, but they are not breaking Moses' law;
they are not under Moses' law. Christians, however, are bound to God's law by virtue of its
expression in the New Testament, apart from the
national and theocratic characteristics of the Mosaic codification which were unique to Israel.
God has not changed; He is still the God of love
in the New Testament. And the moral principles
which express His love to us and show us how
to express it to God and others are still the same.

THE RELATION OF LAW AND LOVE

Whenever one speaks of laws expressing the
love of God and one's love to God and others,
he is invariably confronted with the cry of legal-
ism. Are laws and love incompatible? Is one
necessarily legalistic because he believes in many
universally binding moral laws? The New Testament provides a negative answer to these questions.

Jesus never replaced the laws of Moses with a
single law of love as some have suggested. First
of all, Jesus never said that there was only one
law of love. He spoke of at least two laws of love,
one for loving God and one for loving other men
(Matt. 22:38, 39). Furthermore, Jesus never said
these were to be *substituted* for the many moral
laws embodied in the Old Testament, but were
merely a *summary* of them. Jesus explicitly denied
that He was proposing a new morality. "Think not
that I have come to abolish the law," He de-

clared, "I have come not to abolish them but to
fulfill them" (Matt. 5:17). Likewise, the apostle
John wrote, "I am writing you no new commandment, but an old commandment which you had
from the beginning." And "this is the message
which you have heard from the beginning, that
we should love one another . . ." (1 John 2:7;
3:11). The law of love summarized but does not
antiquate the many moral laws contained in the
Old Testament and which are restated in the New
Testament.

The summary of the many laws into two is described by several phrases in the New Testament.
Jesus said, "On these two commandments *depend*
("hangeth," asv) all the law and the prophets"
(Matt. 22:40). After stating the Golden Rule
Jesus said, "this is *(the essence of)* the law and
the prophets" (Matt. 7:12). In the Sermon on
the Mount He spoke of *"fulfilling"* the law and
prophets (Matt. 5:17). Paul uses this later word
saying, "the whole law is *fulfilled* in one word,
'You shall love your neighbor as yourself'" (Gal.
5:14). In parallel with the word "fulfilled" Paul
speaks of the second table of the Ten Commandments being *"summed up* in this sentence, 'You
shall love your neighbor as yourself'" (Rom. 13:
8, 9). In brief, the love commandments do not
replace the Ten Commandments; they only reduce
them to their common essence, love. The two
commandments of love merely summarize the
many moral laws. All of the many laws depend
on love as their foundation and are fulfilled by
love in their manifestation. The laws of God and
love are not incompatible; they fit like hand and
glove.

The laws spell out love in its many spheres.

Each commandment is love put into operation in a given sphere of human relationship. The command not to kill is saying in essence that so far as *one's relationship to another innocent human life* is concerned it is never the loving thing intentionally to snuff it out. The command not to commit adultery is saying *so far as one's relationship to his neighbor's wife is concerned* it is never the loving thing to have intercourse with her. And so on. Each commandment spells out love in a given sphere. Each law is love put into words which will guide one in the loving course of action.

There is a distinct advantage in spelling out love in each of the basic relationships of life, as opposed to giving one contentless principle and instructing men to go and "love." What does love mean in this or that sphere? they could rightly ask. Would this be a loving relationship? Or, could desiring my neighbor's possessions be a loving attitude? Once love is spelled out in its many spheres, a man is provided with concrete answers to these questions. The laws define the duty of love in each sphere of responsibility. It is permissible to summarize the many laws into the law of love, but this summary is an insufficient guide to the many areas of life unless one is aware of the specific laws of which this is the summary. It is incredible to give a man a summary of a story he has never read and then ask him to write the whole story. God in His wisdom spelled out the story (in the many moral principles of the Old and New Testaments) which is summarized in the love principle. The summary is necessary so that we do not forget that love is the heart of each command. But the many laws are necessary so that we have a sufficient understanding of what are the responsibilities of love in the various spheres of human relationship. God did not leave it for us to guess about the meaning or the application of love to human relationships. He spelled it out in clear and simple words, "You shall do this," and "You shall not do that."

The fact that many of the commandments are negative in form does not mean they are negative in intent. It is much easier to name the few things which are not loving than the many things which are. In effect the commandments are saying that some things are never loving and should be avoided. Everything else can be loving and it is our obligation to see that it is loving. Further, the intention behind the negative commandments is positive, viz., love is the only way to treat others. And God was so concerned that we know exactly what it means that He spelled out the meaning of love in His laws. The law is love put into words.

Chapter 6

Christ: Putting Love Into Life

The law put love into words so that men could understand its meaning. Christ put love into life so that men could fulfill its demands. Jesus said the relation of His life to the law was one of fulfillment (Matt. 5:17). It is this filling up or bringing to perfection the moral principles contained in the Old Testament which the life of Christ personifies and which it will exemplify in the life of the believer.

CHRIST: THE PERFECTION OF THE LAW

Human nature is such that a life is more impressive than word, especially in the realm of ethics. When it comes to knowing and doing what is right there is no substitute for a living example. Christ was that example. He personified all the moral precepts contained within the Old Testament. His life was an exemplification of the entire Mosaic legislation. Jesus not only taught the moral law of God but He lived it to perfection. He lived a life truly worth watching.

What Jesus manifested in His life was the love of God. As John observed, "In this the love of God was manifest among us, that God sent His

only Son into the world, so that we might live
through Him" (1 John 4:9). Christ was God's
love gift wrapped in human flesh. He was the
Word about God's love in our world. "The Word
became flesh and dwelt among us," declared John
(John 1:14). The law of Moses was an expression
of God's love in words. The Incarnation of Christ
is an expression of God's love in human life.

The Bible is very explicit as to the perfection
of Christ's life. Peter said, "He committed no sin;
no guile was found on his lips" (1 Peter 2:22).
He was "a lamb without blemish or spot" (1:19).
Paul said Christ "knew no sin" (2 Cor. 5:21).
Hebrews tells us that Christ was one "who in
every respect has been tempted as we are, yet
without sinning" (4:15). John's first letter has
numerous references to Christ's sinlessness. We
know that "in him is no darkness at all" (1:5).
He is "Jesus Christ the righteous" (2:1). Further,
"he is pure" (3:3) and "in him there is no sin"
(3:5). Pilate said, "I find no crime in this man"
(Luke 23:4). Such has been the verdict of history: Jesus lived a truly flawless life.

The perfection of Christ's life was not simply
in the absence of any wrong; it was in the presence
of the good in Him, particularly of His love.
Jesus loved God the Father (John 14:31); He
loved His disciples (John 13:1); He showed compassion on the multitudes (Mark 8:2) and particularly His own people who rejected Him (Matt.
23:37). His life was in fact one continual story
of love. He healed the sick, opened the eyes of
the blind, raised the dead and spent Himself tire-
lessly in helping others.

Several important aspects of divine love are
dramatically illustrated in Christ's life. First, He

loved *indiscriminately*. Others would have avoided
the woman of ill-repute at the well. Jesus made
it a point to help her (John 4). Christ also loved
unconditionally. Even though He knew from the
beginning that Judas would betray Him (John 13:
11), nevertheless, He manifested the same concern
for him as He did the other disciples (cf. John 6:
71; 13:1; 17:12). Further, the love of Christ was
incomparable. For His crucifiers He prayed,
"Father, forgive them; for they know not what
they do" (Luke 23:34). As Paul said, "one will
hardly die for a righteous man," but "God shows
His love for us in that while we were yet sinners
Christ died for us" (Rom. 5:7, 8). Finally, the
love of Christ was *immeasurable*. Paul prayed for
understanding of "what is the breadth and length
and height and depth, and to know the love of
Christ which surpasses knowledge" (Eph. 3:18).

The essence of Christ's love is that it was a
sacrificial love. "For God so loved the world that
He gave . . ." (John 3:16). In like manner the
apostle spoke of Christ "who loved me and *gave
himself* for me" (Gal. 2:20). Jesus had told His
disciples, "Greater love has no man than this, that
a man lay down his life for his friends" (John
15:13). Claiming to be the good shepherd, He
said, "*I lay down my life* for the sheep . . . No
one takes it from me, but I lay it down of my
own accord" (John 10:15, 18). John wrote, "by
this we know love, that he *laid down his life* for
us" (1 John 3:16). Christ's love is supreme and
sacrificial love, for it was with the supreme sacrifice of His own life that He manifested it to the
world.

Christ's love is not only sacrificial but it was
an *involved* love. He was not afraid to be in

contact with sinners. He attended a wedding
(John 2); He enjoyed banquets with tax collectors
and sinners (Matt. 9:9); He even carried the repu-
tation of being "a friend of tax collectors and
sinners" (Matt. 11:19). Jesus touched the leper
He healed (Mark 1:41); He talked with the harlot
at the well (John 4); He mingled with the crowds,
attended the holiday feasts, and went regularly
to the temple and synagogue. Jesus was a "mixer"
who was not afraid of contact with the world.
One of His parables illustrates His involved love
most beautifully. The Good Samaritan found the
man beaten and robbed by thieves and *came to
where he was;* and when he saw him, he had
compassion, and went to him and bound up his
wounds, pouring on oil and wine." And after get-
ting him a motel room, he said to the manager,
"Take care of him; and whatever more you spend,
I will repay you when I come back" (Luke 10:
33-35). So it was with the love of Christ. His
was an unsolicited concern and an involved compassion for the lives of men. Here is a love so
divine it can forgive those who crucify him and
yet so human it can cry at a friend's funeral (John
11:35). Christ's love was so transcendent that it
could not be measured and yet so down to earth
that harlots and tax collectors could experience
it. No wonder the hymnal is filled with songs on
the love of God.

Christ's love was also *firm.* He was not unloving when He rebuked the Pharisees for their
hypocrisy, warning, "Woe to you, scribes and
Pharisees, hypocrites! . . . Woe to you blind
guides . . . Woe to you, scribes and Pharisees,
hypocrites! for you are like whitewashed tombs
. . ." (Matt. 23:13, 16, 23, 29). Nor was Christ

unloving to warn men of the fire of hell (Matt. 5:22; 18:8). It would have been less than kind to leave men with the impression there are no consequences for their sins. Jesus manifested a firmness of love in expelling the money-changers from the temple with a whip: "Take these things away; you shall not make my Father's house a house of trade," He commanded (John 2:16). Love need not be soft to be kind, "for the Lord disciplines him whom he loves, and chastises every son whom he receives" (Heb. 12:6).

CHRIST: THE BELIEVER'S PATTERN

Christ's love was not intended merely as a work of art, that men may behold its beauty and sing its praise. His love is not primarily aesthetic but redemptive and ethical. It is not merely a picture to behold but a pattern to follow. The Scriptures say, "By this we know love, that He laid down His life for us; and we ought to lay down our lives for the brethren" (1 John 3:16). John 3:16 declares God's love for us; 1 John 3:16 demands that we love others in the same manner. Jesus is the pattern for the believer's love responsibility.

The trademark of Christianity is love. "By this all men will know that you are my disciples, if you have love for one another," announced Jesus (John 13:35). Again, "this is my commandment, that you love one another as I have loved you" (John 15:12). The same theme is picked up by Paul when he writes, "walk in love, *as Christ loved us* and gave Himself up for us" (Eph. 5:2). Husbands are told, "love your wives *as Christ loved the church* and gave himself up for her" (Eph. 5:25).

Notice from the foregoing quotations that the Christian's love should be sacrificial, just as Christ's was. "Greater love has no man than this, that a man *lay down his life* for his friends" (John 15:13). In addition, the Christian's love should be forgiving as Christ's was. "Love your enemies and pray for those who persecute you" (Matt. 5:44), Jesus commanded. The apostles repeat the same truth: "Bless those who persecute you . . . Repay no one evil for evil . . . No, 'if your enemy is hungry, feed him; if he is thirsty, give him drink' . . . Do not be overcome by evil, but overcome evil with good" (Rom. 12:14, 17, 20, 21). Stephen's prayer for his assassins as he died a martyr's death was reminiscent of Jesus' prayer: "Lord, do not hold this sin against them" (Acts 7:60). In this first Christian martyr and in thousands after him the love of Christ has come to perfection, in the lives of His followers. The hallmark of Christianity is a sacrificing and forgiving love.

Christian love, like the Savior's, must also be firm. Fathers are to love their children by bringing "them up in the discipline and instruction of the Lord" (Eph. 6:4). In fact, not to discipline is not to love. For, "he who spares the rod hates his son, but he who loves him is diligent to discipline him" (Prov. 13:24). Love, it will be remembered, does not mean doing what people *want* done to them; it means to do them the good they *need* (see Chapter 3). It was in love that Jesus rebuked Peter saying, "Get behind me, Satan! You are a hindrance to me; for you are not on the side of God, but of men" (Matt. 16:23). And it was love by which Peter was later restored after he had denied Christ three times (John 21:15f.). In like manner, it was loving concern which caused the Corinthian Christians to expel an immoral member (1 Cor. 5:5), for "a little leaven ferments the whole lump of dough" (v. 6). And it was love which restored that member after repentance (2 Cor. 2:6). Love is forgiving but it is also firm. Love is not naive and sentimental; it is realistic and strong. The example of Christ's life is more than ample confirmation of this truth.

No analysis of Christian love would be complete without reference to 1 Corinthians 13. From this passage we learn that love is the greatest virtue. "So faith, hope, love abide, these three; but the greatest of these is love" (v. 13). We learn also that one can be a great benefactor or even a martyr and be without love. "If I give away all I have, and if I deliver my body to be burned, but have not love, I gain nothing" (v. 3). It is apparently possible to give and even to die for selfish reasons. Love, to the contrary, is selfless. "Love is not jealous or boastful; it is not arrogant or rude. Love does not insist on its own way" (vv. 4, 5). Love is a "more excellent way" to live than the exercise of the most demonstrative gifts given to the church (12:31). Love never ends; it is eternal.

Perhaps the most effective way to dramatize the meaning of love is to substitute the word "Christ" for the word "love" in the whole passage. To illustrate, "If I have all faith, so as to remove mountains, but have not Christ, I am nothing . . . Christ is patient and kind. Christ is not jealous or boastful. Christ bears all things, hopes all

things, believes all things, endures all things" and
so on. Christ is the embodiment of love. God is
love and Christ is God's love in human flesh.

The value of Christ's example of love is in-
estimable. The law spelled out the meaning of
love but Christ lived it out. The law defined
love but Christ demonstrated it. The meaning of
love — God's love — could not be more perfectly
manifested than in a life of perfect love. Christ's
life "fulfilled" all that the law required. "For God
has done what the law weakened by the flesh,
could not do; sending his own Son in the likeness
of sinful flesh and for sin, he condemned sin in
the flesh, in order that the just requirement of the
law might be fulfilled in us, who walk not according to the flesh but according to the Spirit" (Rom.
8:3, 4). That is, Christ fulfilled the law for us and
He also fulfills it in us. He was the first human
to live out the demands of love perfectly and He
will transfer that power to us by the Spirit. For
"the fruit of the Spirit is love . . ." (Gal. 3:22).

The value of love manifest in the flesh over love
expressed in the law is now evident. The law
can express well the demands of love but it cannot of itself fulfill those demands. The law can
tell us what love ought to do but it cannot do it.
Christ, on the other hand, did it. He fulfilled all
the demands of the law of love. And by virtue
of His love He provides this love for all who are
willing to receive it. That is, all who are willing
to die to self and allow God's love to flow through
them to others will receive the power to love as
Christ loved. They can say with Paul, "I have
been crucified with Christ; it is no longer I who
live, but Christ who lives in me; and the life I now
live in the flesh I live by faith in the Son of God,

who loved me and gave himself for me" (Gal. 2: 20). Christ's love is more than a pattern for our life; it is the very possibility and power enabling us to live a life of perfect love. John said, "he who loves is born of God and knows God" (1 John 4:7). No one expresses God's love who is not God's child. And no one is God's child except by Christ who loved him and died for him.

Chapter 7

The Alternatives of Love

Love is of God and God is love. Hence, in God there is no conflict of love. There is perfect harmony between Lover (the Father), His Beloved Son and the Spirit of Love between them. On earth it is a different matter. Love seems to find itself in conflict. Duties clash and responsibilities overlap. This confuses the situation for love. What should one do when neither course seems to be the loving thing to do? Sometimes two or more of the commandments conflict; what then?

The people of God have often faced ethical dilemmas. It is wrong to kill his son and it is wrong to disobey God; what should Abraham have done when God told him to sacrifice Isaac (Gen. 22)? God commands obedience to the king, but the king commands the murder of innocent male children. What should the Hebrew midwives have done (Exod. 1)? The Scriptures enjoined obedience to parents but one's parents insist that he not serve God. What is the responsibility of love (Matt. 10:37)? The Bible forbids lying but the lives of God's servants can be saved by doing so. What should Rahab have done (Joshua 6)? The Queen commands that all God's

The Alternatives of Love 63

and hides one hundred of them. Was Obadiah
right (1 Kings 18:13)?

Or, take some other illustrations from the Bible.
A man fears for the safety of his wife. He lies to
protect her, saying she is his sister. Was this the
loving thing for Abraham to do (Gen. 20:12)?
Another man vows to sacrifice to God for victory
over his enemies the first thing that meets him
on returning home. His only daughter met him
at the door. Should Jephthah have sacrificed
her (Judges 11)? The king is mortally wounded;
he requests his servant to kill him with a sword.
Should Saul's armor-bearer have refused (1 Sam.
31)? These situations are not as rare as one
might think, either in the Bible or in present-
day life. How should the Christian love ethic
face them? What are the alternatives within an
absolute ethic of love?

The First Way: There Is Only One Absolute Duty of Love

One way to face the issue is to claim that there
is only one absolute duty and, hence, there is no
conflict. * It takes two absolutes to have an absolute conflict. If there is only one absolute love
norm, then all conflicts are apparent but not real.
In each situation there is only one absolute duty,
viz., do the most loving thing possible.

Several things are significant about this alternative. First, it is simple. The believer is not

* Rather than pin these positions on any exponents, living
or dead, they will be presented here as hypothetical positions.
In this way they can be presented at their best without yield-
ing to the temptation to criticize them because of the way in
which they are presented by a given exponent.

overloaded with the baggage of numerous ethical commandments which are many times in conflict with each other. Second, it preserves the absolute nature of love. God is absolute love and the believer is called upon in each situation to perform the most god-like (i.e., the most loving) deed. Third, this view is situational in that the action of love takes into consideration varying situations. The general rule is to love, but what this means in particular will be determined by the specific situation.

The situations listed above must each be examined in view of one question: what would have been the most loving thing for the individual to do? No doubt it was more loving for the midwives to save the innocent children. No doubt it was more loving for Rahab to lie to save the spies' lives. One cannot always be sure in some situations but he must do his best to discover what is most loving and never do what he does not at least intend as the most loving thing he can do in that situation.

How does one know what love means? He discovers it through the life of Christ and the laws of love stated in Scripture. None of these, however, is absolute in itself. Each merely contributes to an overall impression or intuition of love which is the only thing applied to the specific conflicting situations. Indeed, how else could one resolve conflicts between given commandments unless he appealed to some one overall principle to which even these commandments are subject? Each of the Ten Commandments is not an absolute obligation of love. Rather, each is a general principle, spelling out what is usually the loving thing to do. But it is alleged that sometimes love will demand that one lie or commit adultery or even kill or deny God. For if one could save lives by doing any of these, then surely love would demand that the commandment be broken.

This view has much to commend it, but even in its best form it falls short of a truly Christian love ethic. There are several fatal difficulties. First, there is not just one duty of love. There are at least two, love God and love other men (see Chapter 3). And these two sometimes come into conflict, as the cases of Abraham-Isaac and obedience to God vs. parents demonstrate. As long as the duties of love are on two levels in a sinful world there will be conflicts. And it will not do to say there is no absolute duty to love other men. Christ commanded to the contrary. For what makes the love of neighbor an absolute duty is that it comes as a commandment of God based in His very nature as love. To say there is only one duty, viz., to love God, is to evade the fact that this God commands that one of the fundamental ways of loving Him (vertical) is by keeping His commandments (horizontal). Jesus said, "If you love me, you will keep my commandments" (John 14:15, cf. 1 John 4:20 and Matt. 25:40).

Another serious problem with the one-norm love ethic is that it is too general to be meaningful. It is a summary of a story which God demands we write correctly but which we are left to guess how to write. To tell a man to "love" in all situations without spelling out what this means is like telling him to do "X" or to "zirkle" when he faces a conflict. None of these symbols has any meaning unless it is defined in laws and/or demonstrated in life. But the commandments and Christ do demonstrate the meaning of love for the Christian. They spell out the absolute nature of divine love. Each commandment indicates clearly what love means in a given human relationship. Without these laws and Christ's life the Christian would not know what the absolute obligations of love really are, to say nothing of being able to perform them. He would be left to his own subjective intuitions and guesses.

The Second Way: There Is Always A Third Alternative for Love

A widely held view among Christians, and one which has much more to commend it than the former, is the position that moral conflicts are false dilemmas. In each case there is always a third alternative. One is never forced to do something less than loving, because all the alternatives are not evil. Rahab did not need to lie to save the lives of the spies. God could have preserved her from facing the question or could have delivered the spies from their captors, even if she told the truth. Then, too, silence, even to the point of sacrificing one's own life, is always a third possibility. God is faithful to those who are faithful to His law and will always "with the temptation also provide the way of escape . . ." (1 Cor. 10:13). God intervened and saved Abraham from having to kill Isaac and He would do the same for anyone else who is faithful to His commands, as was Abraham.

Some obviously appealing features about this view emerge upon analyzing it. First, it maintains without compromise the many absolute commands of love in Scripture. There is no evasive attempt to reduce all the many absolute commands of God to a single, virtually meaningless and unusable norm. Second, there is an earnest attempt made to seek third alternatives to breaking any commandment. The assumption is that if God commanded both, then He expects us to keep both and He will see to it that we are able to keep His commandments without sinning. All of this is commendable. One can, so to speak, have his cake of many absolutes and eat it too, knowing that they never really conflict.

But that is precisely where the rub lies. Are all conflicts merely apparent? Is there really always a third way out? The evidence is to the contrary. True, Abraham did not have to kill Isaac, but he did have to *intend to obey God by doing so.* And Jesus taught that morality is a matter of intent (Matt. 5:22, 28). The Hebrew midwives saved the children's lives but they had to disobey God's command to obey the government to do so. And even if some of the commands of God are less than absolute, surely the Ten Commandments would be candidates for absolutes. Yet Jesus pointed out real conflicts between the first and fifth commandments. When a parent commands a child to show his love for the family by denying the true God, what third alternative does the child have? It seems overly optimistic and a bit naive to hold in the face of innumerable cases both in and outside the Bible that there never are any real conflicts. *

A further problem with the third-alternative position has already been implied. Do all commandments have the same force? Are there some

* See Joseph Fletcher, *Situation Ethics: The New Morality,* for many illustrations of conflicts.

higher relationships which take precedence over lower ones? Do all the commandments stand on the same footing? The answer, as we will see shortly, is negative. Some things are of higher value than others. There are different levels and spheres of love. And when there is conflict between them, then one must give way to another. But if this is so, then the position that there are many absolute commandments all equally binding on the believer is untenable. For when equally-binding commands conflict, then the alternatives for this position would necessitate breaking one of the commands. But if one must be broken then the position is invalidated. For in that case there was a real conflict with no real third alternative.

Another objection to the third alternative view is that in order to evade the dilemmas forced by conflict situations it engages in a redefinition of a lie. In this way it can pronounce what would otherwise have been a lie to be morally justified in certain circumstances. For instance, the Bible condemns intentional deception (Prov. 14:25; Zeph. 3:13; 2 Tim. 3:13; Titus 1:10), but both Elisha (2 Kings 6) and Joshua (Joshua 8) were pronounced blameless for deliberately misleading others. The specious grounds for not calling these intentional deceptions lies is that it is a "fallacious assumption that to be truthful we must *under all circumstances* speak and act in terms of the data which come within the purview of others who may be concerned with or affected by our speaking or acting." * The obvious ques-

---

* See John Murray, *Principles of Conduct*, Grand Rapids: Wm. B. Eerdmans Publishing Co., 1957, 1971.

tion is how do we know under what circumstances an intentional deception is justified? Certainly one does not let the situation determine when it is right to lie and when it is not, for then his ethic is no longer normative in the absolute sense but it is purely situational. On the other hand, if there is a higher law in view of which one decides when it is right to intentionally deceive, then he has admitted that the conflict is real and must be resolved by an appeal to the priority of one of the two laws over the other and not by an alleged third alternative. In either case, the fact that conflict situations force one to *do otherwise* than he would have done were he not faced with the conflict shows that there is really no way to perform his obedience to both commands in the same way which he would have done were he not faced with the conflict. For example, Daniel would have otherwise obeyed the king's command, if it had not conflicted with his command to pray only to God (Dan. 6). Likewise, the three Hebrew children (Dan. 3) and the apostles (Acts 4, 5) would have done otherwise were it not for the real conflict between obeying the governmental authorities ordained of God and the commands against idolatry and to preach the Gospel. Surely Abraham would not have otherwise intended to kill his son Isaac, but the real conflict occasioned by God's higher command preempted this duty to preserve his son's life.

There is one more difficulty with the view that denies the reality of moral conflicts. It often tends to be legalistic and/or unmerciful. This is especially true in the forms of this position which refuse to engage in any kind of redefinition of moral principles in view of certain circumstances. Emmanuel Kant would refuse to intentionally deceive a criminal in order to save the life of his would-be victim. Despite the biblical examples to the contrary (Joshua 2 and 1 Kings 18), many Christians follow Kant. In so doing they appear to be saying by their actions that their duty to tell the truth to the guilty is greater than the duty to save the life of the innocent. This seems clearly an unmerciful action. In fact, many of these same people leave lights on in their homes while they are away in order to deceive would-be thieves. Surely it is not right to deceive in order to save one's own property but wrong to deceive to save another's life! In like manner, it seems evidently unmerciful to yield to the demand of a madman to return his borrowed gun so that he can kill his wife. Certainly the law of mercy preempts the man's rights to his own property. Such are the dilemmas created by insisting that there are third alternatives when there are really only two and when one insists on not subordinating one obligation to the higher one. What happens more often than not is that the higher obligation to show mercy is neglected by a wooden insistence on keeping a lesser command. It is precisely these kinds of neglect against which Jesus spoke so often and so forcefully in the Gospels (see Matt. 23:23).

Third Way: Performing the Least Non-Loving Act

There is another way to maintain an absolute ethic of love without sacrificing the universally binding nature of biblical commands. One may simply admit that there are real conflicts between some absolute commands. Sometimes there is no loving possibility open to a Christian. In this event one must simply do the least non-loving thing available. This is an evil world and tragic moral dilemmas are part of this kind of world. The best one can do sometimes is the least evil possible. This position is popularly called the "lesser of two evils" view. In terms of a Christian ethic of love it contends that when there is no way to express love (i.e., no way *not* to break one of the absolute love commandments), then all that remains is to do the least non-loving thing in that situation.

Of course, when one breaks a commandment of God he is guilty. But sin is sometimes unavoidable. The love of God provides forgiveness for those who confess, but the providence of God does not always provide a way to escape sinning. Sometimes there is no third alternative to breaking a commandment. The laws of God are absolute and ought never be broken. But the world is sinful and it is occasionally necessary to break one of God's laws, even for the most godly of believers. When one is confronted with this undesirable conflict, he must decide which is the lesser of the two evils and act accordingly.

Several things commend this view. First, like the previous view, it has the advantage of preserving intact the absolute nature of biblical commands. There are no exceptions to God's imperatives to love under any circumstance. It is always wrong to lie and to kill, etc. If these conflict, then so be it, one must do the lesser evil and lie to save his life. A second advantage is the fact that, unlike the previous position, this view is realistic enough to admit to real conflict situa-

tions. There is no special pleading to divine
providence to provide miraculous third alternatives and no subtle redefining of terms to escape real dilemmas. There are many absolute
commandments and they do sometimes come into
irresolvable conflict with each other.

Each of these points would be valuable in an
absolute Christian ethic, operating in a real but
sinful world. But can we contend for both? Can
an ethic be truly Christian if both of these things
are so? Three forceful arguments indicate a "no"
answer. First, is it consistent with the nature of
an all-wise, all-loving God to hold a man guilty
for doing what was unavoidable? If when a man
cannot avoid sinning, but chooses the lesser evil,
he is pronounced guilty, then God is blaming
him for doing his very best. It does not seem
consistent with the nature of the God of Scripture
to set up absolute but conflicting commands and
then impute guilt to men of good intent, because
they could not avoid breaking the commands
even though they did their moral best. A man is
culpable only if the action was avoidable.

Secondly, there is a most serious problem this
view raises with regard to the sinlessness of Christ.
We are informed that Christ is our moral example,
that Christians should act as He acted. Further,
we are assured that He is our complete moral
example. He faced all the kinds of moral situations we will face. He is "One who in every respect has been tempted as we are, yet without
sinning" (Heb. 4:15). But if there are real moral
conflicts and Jesus faced them, then sinning was
inevitable for Him too. He must have sinned.
But the Bible says clearly that He never sinned
in word, thought or deed (see Chapter 6). It

follows, then, that there are no situations where a lesser evil is called for. There is always a positive good possible. Here, too, evasiveness will not salvage the position. One might be tempted to appeal to some kind of providential sparing of Christ from these moral dilemmas. But this would be to forsake the lesser of evils position for the third alternative view. For if God provided third alternatives for Christ, then why not for us too? Furthermore, if Christ was spared moral dilemmas, then how can He be our example? We have them. Hence, either Christ had irresolvable moral conflicts and sinned, or else He was sinless and there are no situations where the only alternatives are sinful or unloving. Nor does it help to insist that Christ faced no real conflicts because He never sinned to get Himself into these kinds of situations. Neither do other men, for not all moral conflicts are brought on because of one's own previous sins. Some are forced on innocent people by other men. It is in these unavoidable conflicts that it does not make good moral sense to blame either Christ or others for the conflict.

Thirdly, it makes no sense to say one is morally obligated to do the lesser evil. For one cannot be morally obligated to do an evil. But, on the other hand, if one is not morally obligated to do his best (the lesser "evil") then he is free to do the greater "evil," which is also absurd.

THE FOURTH WAY: SUBORDINATING THE LOWER LAWS OF LOVE TO THE HIGHER ONES

Love is never caught on the horns of a dilemma. There are levels and spheres of love and one is always higher than another. Each love command is absolute in its area. But when that area overlaps with another area, then the lower responsibility of love should be subordinated to the higher. When the two conflict, one's duty to God has priority over his duty to his fellow man. The obligation to save an innocent life is greater than to tell the truth to a murderer, and so on. Each of the absolute commandments of the Bible is absolutely binding on the relationship it specifies. There are no exceptions. Adultery is always wrong *as such*. Murder is never right in itself. Lying is universally culpable in and of itself. However, when one or more of these relationships, which are wrong in themselves, overlaps with another area, then one's duty to the lower may be suspended in view of his responsibility to do the higher. There are no exceptions to absolute commands but there are some exemptions in view of higher priorities of love. There is always a greater good.

First, let us distinguish this greater good position from the preceding ones. It differs from the one norm position in that it holds to many norms which are absolutely binding as such. There are no exceptions to universal ethical commands. Further, because there are many laws defining the nature and areas of love, one has meaning, in advance information of what love should do in a given situation. Love is not determined by the situation. Rather, love prescribes what must be done in the situation.

This greater love position is different from the preceding two views as well. In contrast to the third alternative view it holds that God's commandments do sometimes overlap. There are real moral conflicts in which both laws cannot be followed as one normally would. And in contrast to the lesser-of-evils view this position contends that both alternatives of the dilemma are not wrong. God will not hold a man guilty for doing his best. One way is always the morally right way, viz., following the higher command of love.

This greater love position seems to be the most adequate to this writer. It preserves all the values of the other positions and avoids their problems. Of course, it is not without its own difficulties but these are surmountable. Perhaps the most serious problem with this later position is this: how does one know which is the higher law when two conflict? This is where the biblical ordering of the laws of God and the example of Christ play a crucial role. The next chapter will reveal how love operates in following the higher law when there is a conflict of values.

Chapter 8

The Conflicts of Love

The Christian ethic is one of love, love to God and to other men. The laws of God as an expression of God's absolute nature define the meaning of love in the various areas of human relationships. It is never loving as such to murder, to lie, or commit adultery, etc. But these areas sometimes come into conflict with one another. When they do the Christian is obliged to follow the higher love obligation. Beneath each of the conflicting situations is a principle (or principles) indicating which is the highest obligation. The pyramid of principles emerges as the light of God's unchanging love passes through the prism of human experience thereby casting a spectrum or order of God's laws.

1. LOVE FOR GOD vs. LOVE FOR MAN

These principles can be best explained through biblical examples.

In Chapter 3 we saw that love has two basic levels. There is the vertical responsibility to love God with all one's heart and soul and there is the horizontal duty to love one's neighbor as one loves himself. In the event of conflict, the love for God must come first. There are numerous biblical cases to exemplify this principle.

Abraham's love for God was sorely tested by the divine request to sacrifice his beloved son, Isaac (Gen. 22). Walking in unquestioning faith Abraham proceeded to Mt. Moriah with full intent to offer up Isaac. Although God intervened and saved Isaac, the moral decision had been made by Abraham: "God is of more value than my beloved son. If God calls on me to give up the most precious human life I possess, then I will manifest my love to God by giving it to Him." It is well to observe that in no way was Abraham breaking the law of parental concern. Abraham loved Isaac dearly, but he loved God more.

Jesus illustrated the principle of priority of love for God in vivid language. "He who loves father or mother more than me is not worthy of me; and he who loves son or daughter more than me is not worthy of me," He declared (Matt. 10:37). One's love for God should be so strong that his love for relatives will sometimes seem like "hate" by comparison. For "If anyone comes to me and does not hate his own life, he cannot be my disciple" (Luke 14:26). These are hard words, but as the reader was warned at the beginning the Christian love ethic is not for the weak. Even the law of filial piety must be transcended by one's love for God. When Jesus said, "Follow me," and a man hesitated because of parental obligations, requesting, "Lord, let me first go and bury my father," Jesus replied, "Leave the dead to bury their own dead; but as for you, go and proclaim the kingdom of God" (Luke 9:59, 60). One's love for God must supersede his love for his own parents. It should be stressed again that love for God should not be substituted for loving one's parents. Indeed, usually they do not conflict. But when they do, then the highest expression of love possible will be to serve God's orders and not the wishes of one's parents.

Behind these situations is a value principle: *Infinite person is more worthy of love than finite persons.* * Hence, in the event of conflict, the latter must be subordinated to the former.

2. LIFE-SAVING VS. TRUTH TELLING

Not all conflicts involve a clear-cut choice between loving God or loving men. Sometimes the choice is among two spheres in which human love operates. For example, should one lie to save a life? Does love demand that an evil man be told the truth or that an innocent person be protected? In view of the biblical examples one is forced to conclude that lying to save lives is justifiable. Rahab lied to save the men of God from their enemies and God blessed her. It is possible, of course, that Rahab was blessed in spite of, and not because of, her lie. But the lie is not condemned in Scripture and it seems to be an integral part of her faith in God. There are several reasons for believing Rahab's lie was not wrong. First, the Scriptures nowhere condemn her explicitly. Secondly, Joshua commanded that she be saved because "she hid the messengers that we sent" (Joshua 6:17). Now her lie was the essential element in the hiding of the spies. Hence,

---

* Since idols are inhabited by finite evil beings, called demons (1 Cor. 10:20), then all the biblical commands against idolatry support this principle.

in effect she was to be preserved from the judgment of God because she had lied to save the
spies' lives. Thirdly, Rahab hid the spies because
of her faith in God (cf. Joshua 2:9-13 and Heb.
11:31). But here again the lie was the key to
the hiding of the spies. Therefore, it appears that
her lie was actually an expression of her faith
in God. Finally, James informs us (2:25) that
"Rahab the harlot was justified by works when
she received the messengers and sent them out
another way." But only the lie made this possible.
It would follow then that the lie was what en-
abled her to justify her faith in God.

No doubt Obadiah the prophet engaged in
some deceptive activity to save the lives of one
hundred prophets of God (1 Kings 18:13).

An even clearer example is that of the Hebrew
midwives who lied to Pharaoh to cover up their
disobedience to his unjust command to kill the
male children at birth (Exod. 1). The Scriptures
inform us that because they so protected these
innocent lives that "God dealt well with the midwives; and the people multiplied and grew very
strong. And because the midwives feared God
he gave them families" (vv. 20, 21). It seems
evasive to claim that their lie was not an essential
part of their love for these children and for God.

As was said above, those who would never lie,
even to save a life, seem to be inconsistent in
leaving a light on when they leave their homes.
Why are they attempting to deceive a would-be
thief to protect their possessions? Are their household goods more valuable than an innocent life?
Or, what would they do if a mad man with a gun
wanted to know where their loved one was?

Should military leaders, scientists, and intelligence personnel give away the secrets of national security because someone asks? Surely the right of the innocent to live has priority over the right of the guilty to have the correct information.

A maneuver to redefine lying to save a life into a justifiable falsification is an ill-fated semantical move. It is still an intentional falsification which would otherwise have been a lie. Why call it something else only when it is told to save lives? Lying is always wrong as such and never justifiable or right in itself. One is exempt from obedience to the law against lying only when preempted by a greater obligation. Call it what it is — a lie — and then there will not be a tendency to consider it virtuous when it is not in unavoidable conflict with a higher duty.

The principle involved in the priority given to innocent lives is this: *a person not promoting non-loving activity is more worthy of the respect of love than one who is promoting non-loving activity.* Thus, when there is no way to respect the demand of both, then the former must be given deference to the latter. Lying to save an innocent life is not the only application of this principle. More will be illustrated in Chapter 11.

3. LOVE FOR PERSONS VS. LOVE FOR THINGS

Scarcely any principle could be more emphatically taught in Scripture than this: persons are to be loved over things. The person of God, of course, is more valuable than all the things in the world. Jesus warned, "Do not lay up for yourselves treasures on earth . . . You cannot serve God and mammon" (Matt. 6:19, 24). His disciples are not even to be anxious asking, "'What shall we eat?' or 'What shall we drink?' or 'What shall we wear?' For the Gentiles seek all these things . . . But seek first his kingdom and his righteousness, and all these things shall be yours as well" (vv. 31, 33). God is more valuable than the necessities of life. The Bible also says God is more valuable than the gold in His temple (Matt. 23:17, 21) or even the temple itself (Matt. 12:6).

Not only is God greater than the most valuable things in this world but so are men, who have been created in His image. "For what does it profit a man to gain the whole world and forfeit his life" (Mark 8:36)? Nothing in this world, not even sacred things, is as valuable as a human life. David demonstrated this, and Jesus supported it, when He entered the Holy Place and ate the Bread of the Presence (Matt. 12:3, 4). The four who broke through the roof to bring a sick man to Jesus apparently believed that his life was more valuable than the tile on a roof (Mark 2:4). Jesus demonstrated that a human life was more precious than a whole herd of animals when He cast the demons from the man into the swine (Mark 5:11f.). Jesus no doubt implied the principle that people are more valuable than money, even if it is one's tithe, when He said, "you tithe mint and dill and cummin, and have neglected the weightier matters of the law, justice and mercy and faith" (Matt. 23:23). The principle could scarcely be put clearer than Paul did when he wrote, "the love of money is the root of all evils" (1 Tim. 6:10). Things are not to be loved more than people. Things are not even to be loved; they are to be used. People are to be loved.

The principle involved is clear: *persons are to be loved over things.* * Things and people should never be valued equally. Whenever there is a conflict of interest, one should always give people priority over things.

4. LOVE FOR MANY PERSONS VS. LOVE FOR FEW PERSONS

Some truths seem too obvious to need proof. Perhaps this is why it is more difficult to find Scriptural support for the principle that many lives are more valuable than fewer ones than for some other precepts. Nevertheless, the Bible does teach this both by general principle and in specific cases. Samson sacrificed his own life to take many of the enemy, and, hence, save the lives of his people (Judges 16:29, 30). David slew Goliath to protect the many lives of his countrymen (1 Sam. 17:49f.). Caiaphas counseled the Jews by this principle saying, "it was expedient that one man should die for the people" (John 18:14). This was no doubt an unwitting prediction of the principle involved in the atonement wherein Christ gave His life that all men may be saved. Paul was willing to exchange his life for the salvation of his people (Rom. 9:3).

On a broader plane the whole interest of Scripture in spreading and multiplying life supports the principle that many are more valuable than few. God told Adam to "Be fruitful and multiply, and fill the earth" (Gen. 1:28). (The last phrase

* "Things" here should be taken broadly to include activities, rituals, etc. Thus, Jesus' deed of helping people on the sabbath would also illustrate this principle. Helping people is more important than performing one's religious ritual (Matt. 12:10f.).

put limits on the principle, viz. "many" are better than "few" but not better than "too many".) The Gospel is for all men. God is not willing that any should perish (2 Peter 3:9).

Further justification seems unnecessary. However, one qualification is called for. Implied in the illustrations so far has been the fact of *equality of lives*. Of course, many innocent lives are better than few innocent lives or, many of any other equal kinds. But this is not true when the comparison is between the wicked and the righteous. The Bible has numerous examples of a *few* righteous taking priority over *many* wicked. This is why Israel was to exterminate the Canaanites (Lev. 18:25). Noah and his seven relatives were preserved while the rest of the wicked world perished (1 Peter 3:20). In fact, the history of redemption has been the history of the "little flock." God destroyed the many wicked of Sodom and saved only the few righteous of Lot's family, etc.

The principle involved, then, is this: *all other things being equal, love demands that many lives be preferred to few lives*. Often it is possible to save all. But when it is not, then one should save the most he can of the best kind he is able.

5. Love for the Actual vs. Love for the Potential

The Bible lends support to another love principle: *an actual life is to be given the priority of love over a potential life*. The rule seems obvious enough; an oak tree is more valuable than an acorn. A fully developed human is of greater worth than an embryo. In support of the latter is the fact that causing the death of an embryo by miscarriage was not considered a capital crime, as was the taking of a fully developed human life (Exod. 21:22, 23).

The whole stress on the value of growth and maturity in Scripture supports this principle as well (cf. 1 Peter 2:2). The mature is more valuable than the immature; the experienced than the inexperienced (cf. 1 Tim. 3:6). Why develop if the undeveloped is just as good as the developed? The point is too self-evident to labor. However, the principle must be qualified by an "all things being equal" phrase. For when it comes to the choice of a mother vs. an embryo, then this principle would indicate that the mother should be saved. But if the choice were between a mother dying of cancer and the baby she carries, this principle is no longer definitive. Likewise, the principle says nothing about the choice between the infantile and the senile, the sub-human or the post-human. * There is not often a real conflict in these areas as there is with mother and unborn. But in the event of a conflict between unequals this principle does not hold.

6. Potential Persons vs. Actual Things

Brief mention should be made here of a correlative principle to the foregoing one, viz., *a potential person is more valuable than any actual things.* An unborn child is worth more than a

---

* On the question of living "vegetables," one would judge that a potential or undeveloped human (i.e., an embryo) would be of more value because it has a future in which interpersonal relations can be actualized; the living vegetable does not. Of course, there is usually no reason why both cannot live. We are speaking here of a choice *only in the case of an irresolvable conflict.* Both should be saved whenever possible.

fully grown animal, or the world's largest diamond. A potential human being is not a mere tissue or appendage of the human body. None of these grow into men, made in the image of God. The fact that an embryo is less valuable than a mother does not mean that it is less valuable than money. No amount of money is equivalent to a potential human being. In no event should abortion be treated like an appendectomy. Those who tamper with the emerging human life cradled in a mother's womb are intervening with the work of God (Ps. 139:14-16).

Stones do not grow into human beings, whether they be pebbles or jewels. But fertilized human ova do become human beings. Thus, it is a most serious business to snip a budding human life. One must have higher cause than economic or personal inconvenience. No amount of earthly things are worth the sacrifice of a developing human being. These potential persons are of greater value than any mere things in the world.

7. Complete Persons vs. Incomplete Persons

Both complete and incomplete persons are persons and should be loved. Both are fully human and should never be weeded out the way undesirable plants and animals are eliminated. God loves the handicapped, the retarded and all exceptional human beings and we should too. All of this notwithstanding, it is still a fact that, other things being equal, a person with complete mental and physical abilities is more valuable than one without. And although there is rarely a real conflict in which it is necessary to choose one over the other, yet when the choice is called for,

the complete must be considered of more value
than the incomplete.

The very fact that we give special attention to
the disabled and handicapped to make them more
self-sufficient and complete indicates that the latter
state is preferable to the former. Jesus healed the
lame and opened the eyes of the blind, not because their more complete life was less desirable,
but because He too believed that it was better
to be complete. "Wouldest thou be made *whole?*"
Jesus asked the infirm man (John 5:6, ASV). On
another occasion, "the throng wondered, when
they saw the dumb speaking, the maimed *whole*
. . ." (Matt. 15:31). God is not only interested
in our spiritual wholeness (i.e., holiness) but
physical wholeness as well. The superior value
placed on a complete person is seen in the selec-
tion of the priest in the Old Testament. "For no
one who has any blemish shall draw near, a man
blind or lame, or one who has a mutilated face
or a limb too long, or a man who has an injured
foot or an injured hand, or a hunchback, or a
dwarf . . ." (Lev. 21:18-20). The animals given
to God were to be without spot or blemish and
He also placed a higher value on the perfect or
complete human over the incomplete.

Here again the qualification must be understood. *All other things being equal, the complete
is more valuable than the incomplete.* If one had
to choose between a one-armed apostle Paul and
a two-armed Hitler the situation is different. The
cases are unequal and the fourth principle above
would give priority to Paul. This does not mean
that undesirables should be eliminated. Both the
complete and incomplete should be preserved.

However, if both cannot be kept, then the best must be preserved.

In summation, in the ordinary discharge of one's moral duties there is usually no conflict. Usually, all of God's commands can be kept without real conflict. One can love complete and incomplete; he can preserve the actual and the potential; he can save the many and the few. However, in the moral exigencies of our world there arise irresolvable moral conflicts, not of one's own making. And when it becomes obvious that one cannot keep two clashing love responsibilities, then he must choose — he must choose the higher over the lower. This is most demonstrable in the conflict between loving God and loving other men. But also, within one's relationships to other men there are times when one must choose the higher responsibility of love over the lower one.

Chapter 9

The Weightier Matters of Love

There is a persistent myth abroad among Christians that all sins are equal. "Little" sins, "big" sins, all sins are alike in God's eyes, we are often told. It is one of the purposes of this chapter to show that what has already been said about the Christian love ethic is categorically opposed to this myth.

GREATER AND LESSER GOODS

Jesus spoke of the "weightier" matters of the law. Justice and mercy have greater weight on the scale of God's values than does tithing, although the law required both (Matt. 23:23). Helping a human being in need was of more importance to Jesus than "profaning the sabbath" (Matt. 12:5). "God desires mercy more than sacrifice" was Jesus' reply to those who accused Him of breaking the sabbath (v. 7). Again, "the sabbath was made for man, not man for the sabbath" (Mark 2:27). Not only did Jesus heal on the sabbath but His disciples would "pluck ears of grain" to satisfy their hunger. Jesus referred to these activities as "guiltless," "lawful" and doing "good" (Matt. 12:7, 12). They were not a lesser evil but a positive good, in fact, a greater good than keeping the letter of the sabbath law.

Several lines of evidence indicate that not all moral matters are weighted equally by God. First, there are the two great levels of duty for love (discussed in Chapter 3); second, the conflicts between higher and lower laws (treated in the previous chapter) indicate some things are greater goods than others; finally, there are numerous specific references in the Bible to greater and lesser goods and evils.

As to the two levels of love, Jesus most emphatically taught that it is greater to love God than man. It is called the *"first"* and the *"great"* commandment as opposed to the "second" (Matt. 22:38, 39). In another place Jesus referred to the *"least"* of God's commandments (Matt. 5:19). "He who loves father or mother more than me is not worthy of me," Jesus affirmed (Matt. 10:37). Love for God must be *"with all your heart,* and with all your soul, and with all your mind" whereas love for neighbor is merely *"as yourself."* The difference indicates how much greater one's love for God should be. To further illustrate, one's love for God can sometimes lead him to disobey his parents (if, e.g., they command him to sin), but one's love for parents should never lead one to disobey God under any circumstance.

In each of the conflict situations discussed in the preceding chapter there was always a greater good. Persons have greater value than things; many persons are more valuable than few persons; good people are better than evil men; actual persons take priority over potential persons, etc. If both choices were equally good, then either alter-

native one took in a conflict between them would
be right. And if both were equally evil then
nothing one does in these situations would be
good. But there is a good alternative, viz., following the greatest good in each conflict. Thus,
the conflict situations manifest a hierarchy of
good and evil in which there is always a greater
good to be performed.

Specific support for the truth that not all actions
are equally good or equally evil is found throughout the entire Bible. The whole concept of re-
wards is built on the premise that some deeds
are better than others. This is why some receive
a crown and some do not (Rev. 3:11). This is
why when our works are tested what remains
will be "gold, silver, precious stones" for some
or "wood, hay, stubble" for others (1 Cor. 3:12).
There is an obvious difference of value intended
here. The same concept of a scale of values is
brought out by Jesus' commendation to His servants. One who did greater good was told, "Well
done, good servant! . . . you shall have authority
over *ten cities.*" The other servant who did a
lesser good was informed, "And you are to be
over *five cities*" (Luke 19:17, 19). Paul spoke of
love being the *"greatest"* virtue (1 Cor. 13:13)
and Jesus referred to giving one's life for another
as *"greater* love has no man than this" (John 15:
13). In brief, as Paul wrote, "We must all appear
before the judgment seat of Christ, so that each
one may receive good or evil, according to what
he has done in the body" (2 Cor. 5:10).

Men will be rewarded according to the degree
of good they have done and they will be judged
according to the degree of evil they have per-

formed. John wrote, "And the dead were judged
. . . by what they had done" (Rev. 20:12). Not
only are deeds rated in degrees of evil, but
thoughts are as well. Jesus distinguished three
levels of evil thought against one's brother: "Everyone who is *angry* with his brother shall be
liable to judgment; whoever *insults* his brother
shall be liable to the council, and whoever says,
'You *fool!*' shall be liable to the 'hell of fire'"
(Matt. 5:22). The cities of Chorazin and Beth-
saida were worse sinners than Sodom, declared
Jesus. "But I tell you that it shall be *more toler-
able* on the day of judgment for the land of
Sodom than for you" (Matt. 11:24). In a very
clear passage Jesus declared to Pilate, "he who
delivered me to you has the greatest sin" (John
19:11). Paul called himself "the foremost of sinners" (1 Tim. 1:15) and Jesus labeled one sin
unforgivable (Matt. 12:32). Some Christians at
Corinth had sinned enough to be "weak and ill"
but others enough to have "died" (1 Cor. 11:30).
John speaks of a sin so bad that it is *"mortal"*
(1 John 5:16).

In view of all the Bible teaches on greater and
lesser evils the myth that all sins are equal is untenable. All sins are sin, but not all sins are equally sinful. And James' statement that "whoever
keeps the whole law but fails in one point has
become guilty of all of it" (2:10) is not contrary
to what has been said here. James did not declare that all were *equally* guilty. He is not speaking about the equality of sin but the unity of the
law. Whoever breaks God's laws, whichever one
he breaks, is a lawbreaker. James does not say
that all men are equally lawless. In fact, James

too recognized greater and lesser goods when he wrote, "he who teaches will be judged with greater strictness" (3:1). Neither did Jesus affirm that all sins are alike when He taught "that every one who looks at a woman lustfully has already committed adultery with her in his heart" (Matt. 5: 28). This passage does not teach that thinking adulterous thoughts is no better than thinking about lying or killing. What it says is that sin springs from the heart. It does not even teach that "It is just as bad to think it as to do it." Jesus did not affirm that lust is the same as adultery but only that lust was committing adultery *in one's heart*. To commit it *with one's body* is even a worse sin, for it has social consequences which mental lust does not.

Let us draw some conclusions from these data about good and evil. First, it is evident that there are degrees of good and evil. Some acts are better and some are worse than others. Good and evil are ranked in a pyramid with the best at the top and the worst on the bottom and varying degrees of good and evil in between. Second, some single moral acts are more vicious than numerous other acts of evil. For example, one brutal act of murder can be more evil than a hundred little lies. Third, whenever there is a conflict among good alternatives or between good and evil, then the morally right course of action is always the greatest good or the most loving thing to do. A man who could have rescued five drowning people actually did evil by only saving two of them. To do less than the best possible is an evil. Finally, in view of the relative values of different moral acts, it is necessary for the Christian to "weigh" the alternatives for love. This is not always easy to do, but the love ethic never promised to be an easy ethic. Each believer must be informed by Scripture of the divine scale of values and make his ethical decisions accordingly.

WEIGHING THE ALTERNATIVES FOR LOVE

The basis for the ordering of goods according to greater to lesser is the greatest of all goods, God. The Absolute Good is the measuring point for all other goods as related to it. But since God cannot be known directly by mortal man (Exod. 33:20f.; John 1:18), He is made known through His law and in His Son. Thus, the inscripturated truth about the absolute God is the criterion for measuring greater and lesser goods. God is absolute love and what this means is spelled out for us in His laws and in the life of Christ revealed in the gospels. The value of an act, then, is determined by how Christ-like (which is god-like) it is. Some acts are more Christ-like or godly than others. Hence, ethical priorities are determined by how far the acts are from the point of absolute love. The more god-like the greater the good; the closer the resemblance to Perfect Love the more loving the act is.

Knowing which principles are higher and which are lower, based on their proximity to Absolute Love, is only half the ethical battle; the other half is putting these principles into practice. But knowing the laws of God and how they rank in God's measurements is the most fundamental part of the battle. Finite men of good intent will sometimes disagree as to *which* action is the greater good, but there should be no disagreement on *what* constitutes the greater good, nor why it is greater.

This points up a major difference between the absolute ethic of love expounded in these pages and many other contemporary ethics. The Christian ethic is determined by the revealed *rules,* not by the anticipated long-range *results.* The love ethic of Jesus is not utilitarian. Since the days of Jeremy Bentham and John Steward Mill it has been common to speak of determining what is ethically right by estimating what will bring "the greatest good to the largest number of people in the long run." Or, in even more recent terms, what will bring "the greatest amount of love to the most people over the long haul." Despite the superficial similarity in the use of some terms, there are essential differences between a utilitarian love ethic and a biblical one. Both, of course, are concerned with results, even long range results. Both employ principles or norms in deciding what is the greatest good. But the similarities end there.

The differences are most crucial. First, in the Christian ethic of love the long range results are left to God. Man is responsible only for the intended immediate results of choices. God has revealed the rules which will bring the best long range results. We are to follow the rules and God will take care of the final results. In brief, we do not determine what the rule is to be by the results; the results will be determined by the rule. The ethical principles are to decide the pragmatic consequences, not the reverse. Second, utilitarian rules are not absolute. They are generalizations built up on past human experience which serve as guides to achieving the greatest results. Christian ethical principles, on the contrary, are rooted in the nature and will of God. As such they are universally applicable and absolutely binding. They are not generalizations which may admit of unspecifiable exceptions. God's absolute commandments have no exceptions and provide exemptions only when there is clearly a higher commandment conflicting with it. Third, an action is good for a utilitarian only if it brings good consequences. No act has any intrinsic good. If the attempt to rescue a drowning man fails to yield any good results, then the act was not a good act, even though it may have been performed with the best intentions. Not so for the Christian. The loving attempt to rescue a drowning man is good in and of itself whether or not the result is the desired one. God judges an act to be intrinsically good if it was intended to be in compliance with His commands, not because of the extrinsic consequences.

These differences have important repercussions for ethical decisions. The Christian makes no decision on *what* is right and what is wrong; God has already decided that and revealed it to men. The Christian decides only *which* thought or action will be in accord with what is revealed to be right. Further, the Christian does not have to intuit what is the loving thing in a conflict situation. Which principles are higher and which are lower has also been revealed. Finally, Christians do not have to resort to long range guessing based on human experience to know what is the best thing to do. The Christian knows which course of action will *here and now* fulfill the higher norm; the long range results are left to God.

However, the Christian ethic is not "signed, sealed and delivered" by God in neat little packages of rules which demand no struggle and decision by the believer. On the contrary, the Christian ethic of love demands the greatest dedication. The Christian needs to know the Scriptures to know God, His laws and the exemplary life of His Son. It was Jesus who charged the religious people of His day, "You are wrong because you know neither the scriptures nor the power of God" (Matt. 22:29). Further, the Christian must be involved directly in weighing the alternatives to determine his course of action, which action will be most in accord with the scriptural commands. Finally, the Christian must act on his ethic. Merely knowing the path of love is not sufficient; the Christian must *take* that path in a world of indifference and hate. Indeed, the Christian love ethic by its very nature calls for deep and personal involvement; for it is of the essence of Christ's love to be deeply and personally involved with human needs.

The Role of the Holy Spirit

By stressing the necessity of personal decision-making it should not be concluded that the role of the Holy Spirit is being slighted. In ethical truth, as in all other truth, it is the Holy Spirit who reveals it to the Christian and the Holy Spirit who enables him to perform it (John 16: 13). Without the Spirit revealed principles for action and the Spirit empowered motivation to perform what is right there can be no truly Christian ethic. However, the biblical Christian is firmly committed to the proposition that the Spirit of God leads through the Word of God and not

by some mysterious supra or extra biblical "radar."
The Bible is sufficient for faith and practice; it
is a complete revelation of God's absolute love.
There are no moral situations which Christians
face for which there are no principles in Holy
Scripture. Nonetheless, it is true that the believer
may be ignorant, dull and/or forgetful of biblical
truth. And it is in correcting these situations that
seeking the guidance of the Holy Spirit is not
only helpful but essential. In short, when a believer finds himself unable to discover what is
the course of action demanded by God's love,
he must seek the guidance of the Holy Spirit.
The answer may come in different ways. One
may be reminded of a forgotten truth, he may
be directed to a principle heretofore unknown
or he may gain a new insight into ethical norms
he already uses.

But in all of these cases the Spirit is directing
us to the Word for an answer. And in no case
should the believer ever seek to go beyond or
around what is written in the Word of God.
The Spirit of God never leads contrary to the
Word of God (cf. Rom. 8:1f.; 1 Cor. 12:3).

Chapter 10

Love and Life-taking

Perhaps the most difficult challenge facing the Christian is the relation of love and life-taking. Is it ever right to take another human life? Does love ever demand the sacrifice of human beings? What about abortion, mercy-killing, capital punishment and war? These are weighty questions and a true test of the Christian love ethic. For if love is inapplicable to these crucial issues of life today, then it is an unworkable ethic.

Life-taking as Such Is Never Demanded by Love

The intentional taking of another human life is never an act of love as such. "You shall not kill" is in both Old and New Testaments (Exod. 20:13; Rom. 13:9). John said, "as for murderers . . . their lot shall be in the lake that burns with fire and brimstone, which is the second death" (Rev. 21:8). Peter reminded the Christians, "let none of you suffer as a murderer . . ." (1 Peter 4:16). Those who intentionally took the life of another person in the Old Testament received retribution in kind (Exod. 22:23). Following Cain's hateful initiation of the life-taking process (Gen. 4:8), murder ran rampant through the whole

Cainite civilization "and the earth was filled with violence" (Gen. 6:11). God's judgment ensued through the flood.

When Noah and family emerged, God commissioned them with authority to enforce the recognition of the wrongness of murder in these words: "whoever sheds the blood of man, by man shall his blood be shed; for God made man in his own image" (Gen. 9:6). The essential evil of murder is conspicuous in this passage: murder is killing God in effigy. Man is made in the image of God, and whoever takes his life has initiated an assault on God. It was because of the gravity of this offense that murder was considered worthy of capital punishment.

What is even more sobering is the fact that murder is not confined to merely an overt act. According to the Christian ethic, murder can be committed "in one's heart." Jesus said, "You have heard that it was said to the men of old, 'You shall not kill . . . But I say unto you that every one who is *angry* with his brother shall be liable to judgment'" (Matt. 5:22). Adultery springs from lust (v. 28) and murder springs from anger rooted in hate. "For from within, out of the heart of man, come evil thoughts, fornication, theft, murder . . . All these evil things come from within and they defile a man," Jesus declared (Mark 7:21-23). John flatly announced that "anyone who hates his brother is a murderer, and you know that no murderer has eternal life abiding in him" (1 John 3:15). Hence, murder at its very root is diametrically opposed to the Christian ethic of love; murder is hate. And hate is as incompatible with love as light and darkness (see Luke 16:13).

The Christian love ethic never calls upon one to murder. The intentional taking of another's life is as unloving as hate; it is not godlike, for God is love. In fact it is anti-God since it is anti-man who is made in God's image. Love demands that one manifest concern even for his enemies. Jesus commanded, "I say unto you, Love your enemies and pray for those who persecute you" (Matt. 5:44). The apostle repeated, "Repay no one evil for evil. . . . Beloved never avenge yourselves, but leave it to the wrath of God. . . . No, 'if your enemy is hungry, feed him; if he is thirsty, give him drink' . . . Do not be overcome by evil, but overcome evil with good" (Rom. 12: 17-21).

If life-taking is never the loving thing to do as such, if it is contrary to the God of love, then why does this God often either command or sanction the process in which lives are taken? This is a serious question for the Christian love ethic which demands immediate attention.

It should be noted that life-taking is wrong even if the life is one's own. Suicide is at least as wrong as homicide. The ultimate act against one's self is never an act of love for one's self. The command against killing is contrary to the command to love one's self (see Chapter 4). The Christian is commanded to love his neighbor *as himself*. Paul added, "husbands should love their wives as their own bodies. He who loves his wife loves himself" (Eph. 5:29). That suicide would be an act of hating oneself is as clear as that killing one's wife would be an act of hate against her. Love excludes both. The desire to end one's woes is a selfish desire, and selfishness is not love. The "easy" way out is not in this case the most responsible way out. Love never loses all purpose for living. Suicide is a selfish desire to terminate one's own trouble without concern for helping anyone else with his. A man engaged in loving others has no reason to hate his own life. Loving is the cure for killing, whether the object of the hatred is another or one's self.

Life-saving Is Demanded by Love

Life-taking is hateful, but life-saving is loving. Hence, it is an axiom of the Christian love ethic that life-sacrificing is justifiable only if life-saving is thereby accomplishable. Life-taking as such is never the obligation of love, but sacrificing a life to save lives can be demanded by love. Suicide is a case in point.

Love and Suicide

Suicide for one's supposed self interest is never right because it is selfish and lacks a proper love for one's self and for others. Taking one's life "for one's self" is never loving, but sacrificing one's life for another is the highest expression of love. Jesus declared, "greater love has no man than this, that a man lay down his life for his friends" (John 15:13). Indeed Christ Himself exemplified the principle of sacrificing one's life for another. "I lay down my life . . . No one takes it from me, but I lay it down of my own accord" (John 10: 17, 18). Suicide for selfish reasons is always wrong, but what may be called "sacrificial suicide" can be the highest expression of Christ's love.

A word of caution is needed here. Not every apparent sacrifice of one's life "for others" is really an act of love. Paul made this plain in the great love chapter. "If I deliver my body to be burned,

but have not love, I gain nothing" (1 Cor. 13:3).
Even a martyr is not necessarily dying out of love
for others. He may be sacrificing his life out of
obstinate commitment to his own self-centered
cause. Likewise, not every apparent life-sacrifice
is an act of love. There are several examples of
selfish suicides in the Bible. Saul committed suicide (with the help of his armor bearer) "lest
these uncircumcised come and thrust me through
with it, and make sport of me" (1 Sam. 31:4).
The pride of dying at one's own hand as against
the shame of the enemy's hand is hardly a loving
motive. Equally selfish was Abimelech's request
for aid in committing suicide, "lest men say of me,
'A woman killed him'" (Judg. 10:54). Samson,
on the other hand, apparently sacrificed his life
for unselfish reasons. He prayed before he brought
down more of God's enemies in his death than
he did in his life, "O Lord God, remember me,
I pray thee, and strengthen me, I pray thee, only
this once, O God, that I may be avenged upon
the Philistines . . . " (Judg. 16:28). God answered
his request.

The point is this: the only possible thing which
can justify the sacrificing of one's own life is the
intent to save other lives. Samson was concerned
for the lives of his people oppressed by the Philistines. Christ was concerned for the whole world
and came "to give his life a ransom for many"
(Mark 10:45). Paul, likewise, was willing to be
"accursed and cut off from Christ" for the sake
of his Jewish brethren (Rom. 9:2). John exhorted
Christians to follow Jesus' example in "that he
laid down his life for us; and we ought to lay
down our lives for the brethren" (1 John 3:16).

Caiaphas unwittingly expressed the truth when he said, "it was expedient that one man should die for the people" (John 18:14). The Apostle recognized the rarity of one man dying for another but added "though perhaps for a good man one will dare even to die." But as rare as sacrificial love may be, it is the heart of the Christian love ethic. It is not wrong to die for others; it is the highest act of love one can express to another human being. In so doing, however, one is not really *taking* his own life as such; rather, he is *sacrificing* his life for others.

MERCY-KILLING AND LOVE

Love never demands the taking of *one's own life* for "his own sake" (because suicide is not an act *for* one's self but the ultimate act *against* one's self), but does love ever call on one to take the *life of another* for his own sake? What about the man caught in the burning airplane who pleads to be shot? Would not love demand that he be put out of his misery? Surely love demands that he be treated with all the mercy possible, but not that one take his life even at his own request. If it is not loving to take one's own life in suicide, then surely it is not right to help someone else commit suicide. Saul's armor bearer was not justified in aiding Saul in his suicide any more than Saul was in desiring it. Love has a better remedy than life-taking to express mercy to the dying. "Give strong drink to him who is perishing, and wine to those in bitter distress" (Prov. 31:6). In other words, a sedative but not a sword should be given to the dying. He should be shot with tranquilizers but not with bullets. It is more loving that way. For in thus relieving his pain one is showing mercy, as well as recognizing God's sovereignty over life (cf. Deut. 32:39).

Mercy killing as such is always unloving, but what about mercy-dying? The Christian love ethic says "no" to the former but "yes" to the latter. The Bible does not commit the Christian to the all too common understanding of the Hippocratic oath "to keep *life* going as long as possible." Love demands only that one perpetuate *human life* as long as it is lovingly possible, not sub-human and vegetable life. Allowing someone to die mercifully and naturally can be the most loving alternative. And pumping untold dollars and energies into terminal cases can be the most unloving course of action. Injecting medicine to cause or speed death is one thing (and it is morally wrong), but withholding medicine or aids which are artificially perpetuating inhumanities are quite another (and it is morally right).

But how does one know when to pull out the plug? Who decides? And how do we know a case is posthuman or terminal? Are not miracles always possible? These are all very practical and very important questions and, as was suggested in the previous chapter, love must "weigh the alternatives" very carefully and responsibly. First, by "sub-human" we mean the terminal state in which one cannot enter into any distinctly *human* activity, as opposed to purely vegetable or animal activities. Ingestion, digestion, etc., are not (i.e., uniquely) human. But loving and being loved are distinctly human. If the individual is capable of interpersonal relationship, then he must be treated as a human person — with love. If there is any awareness of or expression of love evidenced in the individual, then he still has *human* life and should be given every aid to continue it. If none of the vital "love-signs" are present and the case is medically terminal, then he should be allowed to die mercifully without any further hindrance of the natural process by medical science.

The meaning of "terminal" has two aspects for Christian love. First, it implies there is no more *medical* hope for recovery. This, of course, must be determined by the best medical authorities available. Second, terminal means that there is no more *spiritual* hope for a recovery. God has been consulted by prayer for the sick (cf. James 5:14f.); miraculous recovery has been prayed for fervently and repeatedly (cf. 2 Cor. 12:8). When both the medical prognostication and the spiritual prospects indicate "no hope," and when due allowance has been made for a margin of human error, then it is the demand of love that the medical support of life be withheld and a merciful death be allowed to occur. At this stage, artificial maintenance of an unmerciful life is less loving than allowing a natural and merciful death.

Who should decide? The decision should be a joint one, including any expressed wishes of the dying, the doctor's medical wisdom, the pastor's counsel, all taken into the final determination by the family. In this collective decision there is a greater probability love will be expressed wisely and less possibility for any one person to bear the psychological guilt which could result. (There is no *moral* guilt because it was the right action.)

So far it has been suggested that *taking* another life in the name of mercy to them is not really what love demands but that *permitting a terminally ill person* to die is loving. That is, mercy killing *for its own sake* is wrong, but what about mercy killing *for the sake of others?* If sacrificial suicide is morally right, why not sacrificial mercy-killing? For instance, if there are seven people on a life-raft which will only hold five, should two be sacrificed to save five? On the validity of the principle of love that many lives are more valuable than few (see Chapter 7), it may be that love would be obliged to sacrifice the few for the many. Before assuming that he is faced with a real conflict, however, the Christian would want to explore all possible third alternatives. Pray for help. Each might take turns swimming and/or holding on the sides or, someone might volunteer to jump off in a sacrificial suicide (Christians ought to be the most likely candidates here). If none of these materialize then straws could be drawn. The captain or whoever is the key to saving the lives of those remaining should be saved. (It would not be in love's interest to ask a pilot to bail out of a plane in distress.) And if the fateful do not withdraw voluntarily, then love for the many would demand the sacrifice of the few. The reader was warned earlier and reminded here that love is not always "soft."

Another example of a justifiable mercy-killing or, better, mercy-sacrificing of human life would be a mad man with an automatic weapon shooting down innocent people from the top of a building. In the name of mercy for the many innocent, love may demand the sacrifice of the one guilty. Of course, here as always, it is assumed that all preventative and persuasive methods have been exhausted. Shooting to wound or immobilize may be just as effective and not nearly as drastic in most cases. But when the lives of the innocent many are in the hateful and fateful hands of the guilty few, then love demands activity not passivity.

Love and Capital Punishment

Capital punishment itself, when justly administered, is a kind of mercy-sacrificing of the guilty for the innocent. Contrary to popular sentimentalism, capital punishment is not based on a barbaric disrespect of the individual's life; it can be an essential part of an ethic of love. It is the murderer who has the barbaric disrespect for the worth of an individual life, not the government which justly sentences him. Love demands that we ask this question: for whom should the mercy be shown, the innocent or the guilty? In failing to buy justice by the sacrifice of the guilty for the innocent, we show disregard for proper love and disrespect for the value of an innocent life. Capital punishment was originally instituted because of the lack of respect for man made in God's likeness (Gen. 9:6). It was reinforced in the Mosaic legislation of the Old Testament (Exod. 21:25), recognized by Jesus (John 19:11), and restated by Paul when he reminded the Roman Christians that the ruler "does not bear the sword in vain" (Rom. 13:4).

The only case in the Bible which makes an exception to it occurred when God personally commuted the death sentence on Cain so that Adam would not be called upon to kill his only remaining son (Gen. 4:10f.). And even here the justice of capital punishment was implied in Cain's own expectation of death and in God's insistence that vengeance would be even greater on anyone who killed Cain (vv. 13-15). Jesus did not make an exception to capital punishment for the woman taken in adultery; according to the Law there must be two or three accusers to establish the fact of guilt. But when Jesus asked, "Has no one condemned you?" she replied, "No one, Lord" (John 8:10, 11). It is a serious thing to exact capital punishment, hence, the identity of the murderer must be beyond question and his responsibility for the murder beyond all doubt.

The ill-fated move to make Old Testament principles, as the one involved in capital punishment, contrary to a supposed "New Testament Love principle" has already been treated in the discussion earlier (in Chapter 5). Love is just as much a part of the Old economy as the New. The unchanging God of love revealed Himself as love in both Testaments. The laws which express this love are the same now as they were for Israel. The truth of God's love expressed in the Ten Commandments was not changed by the cross; it was in fact expressed in the cross. Indeed, the same justice of God which demanded a substitutionary sacrifice of Christ, life for life, is at the root of the morality of capital punishment. There was no other way to satisfy God's justice than for Christ to give His life for ours (Mark 10:45; Rom. 3:21f.; 1 Peter 2:24). And there is no other way to satisfy God's justice (and ensure a just and respectful social order) than to insist on life for life. Utter and hateful disregard for the value of individual lives cannot be tolerated by love; love must condemn it. And the same kind of sentimentality which wishes to eliminate capital punishment as inhuman would, if applied consistently, also eliminate the need for Christ's atoning death. The Bible expressly declares there is no other way (Lev. 17:11; Heb. 9:22). Love *wills* what is right whether it *feels* that way or not; human sentiment should not deter divine sanctions.

LOVE AND ABORTIONS

The Bible says virtually nothing about abortion as such. There is only one passage directly related and it concerns a miscarriage. But the Scriptures have much to say about the value of a human life and this does bear directly on the question of abortion. The love principle is clear: "You shall not kill." The problem is this: is abortion murder? The question can only be settled if the status of the unborn can be established. There are three basic answers to this within Christian theology: (1) If the unborn is *fully human,* then abortion is murder and it would be wrong in every case except if it were a sacrificial abortion to save the life of the mother (or some other life or lives); (2) If the embryo is *pre-human* or sub-human, then it should be treated like an appendix and no murder is involved in cutting out either one; (3) If the unborn is *potentially human* but not fully human, then it must be treated with more respect than any mere thing in the world. The basic problem in deciding which position is correct is not an ethical one; it is theological. The ethical principles of love are clear enough: (a) Humans are more valuable than potential humans; (b) Humans are more valuable than mere things; (c) Potential humans are more valuable than mere things (see Chapter 7). The problem in the case of abortion is not in discovering a principle to apply but in deciding on *what* it is to which one is applying the principle: a human, sub-human, or a potential human.

Now on biblical grounds we may safely eliminate the sub-human alternative, for several reasons: (1) Unborn are the work of God (Ps. 139: 13f.); (2) Unborn are sometimes called of God and even filled with the Holy Spirit (Jer. 1:5; Luke 1:15); (3) David spoke of himself being "conceived" in sin (Ps. 51:5). On the other hand, there are some indications that an embryo is not fully human: (1) First, no *capital fine* was exacted for the death of the embryo on the one who caused the miscarriage. But a capital fine was demanded if the mother died as the result of the incident (Exod. 21:22-24). This would seem to imply that a fully human life is of greater value than that of an unborn baby; (2) an embryo does not have fully human functions such as the ability to engage in interpersonal relationships, etc. We may conclude that if the unborn is neither sub-human nor fully human, then it must be potentially and emergently human. The evidence that it is at least potentially human is the fact that given the opportunity to develop it will express the vital "love-signs" of human beings; it will desire to love and be loved, etc. If the theological question can be settled in favor of a potential and emergently human embryo, then the following moral implications ensue: *It must be given every opportunity to develop its full human potential, unless in so doing it would negate the expression of another's full humanity.* In practical terms this would mean: (1) abortion on demand is wrong; (2) most therapeutic abortions are unjustified, unless it is to save the life of the mother (or others); (3) abortion because of rape and/or incest could be right on the grounds that the higher value of love has been violated by a forced conception. It goes without saying that abortion should not be attempted after viability and, when it is called for, the earlier the better. But abortion simply because the baby is unwanted or to control the population is unwarranted. Babies originally unwanted become subsequently wanted by the parents or others. And birth control, not abortion, is a far better way to control the population.

In summation, love never calls for life-taking as such, but it does sometimes call for life-sacrificing. Whether it is one's own life or that of others, there is only one ground which love can justify for ever sacrificing the life of a human being, viz., saving the lives of human beings. Love must not engage in mercy-killing as such but mercy dying and mercy-sacrificing to save others is within love's pale. With regard to abortion the problem is not so much ethical as it is theological. If the unborn is only potentially but not fully human, then abortion would be the loving thing to do only when fully human lives are at stake if the abortion is not performed.

In brief, love has the highest regard for human life in all of its fullness. Love insists on the preservation of what is human, even if sometimes it must lose a battle to win the war.

Chapter 11

Love and War

One of the thorniest problems facing any ethic is the question of war. Does the ethic of Jesus demand, permit or prohibit participation in warfare? This is not an easy question and, as usual, love does not give an "easy" answer. There are two "easy" alternatives sometimes taken by Christians, but neither faces up squarely to the full responsibilities of love as it has been outlined in the preceding chapters.

Love and the Command of One's Government

It is an implication of love that one be submissive and obedient to higher authority. Husbands and wives are exhorted by Scripture to "be subject to one another out of reverence for Christ" (Eph. 5:21). Children are told to "obey your parents in the Lord" (6:1), and citizens are required to be both submissive and obedient to their governments. Paul wrote, "let every person *be subject* to the governing authorities. For there is no authority except from God, and those that exist have been instituted by God. Therefore he who resists the authorities resists what God has appointed . . ." He then added, "pay all of them

112

their dues. . . . Owe no one anything, except to love one another" (Rom. 13:1, 2, 8). In other words, the only obligation we have to others is to love them, and this implies that we will be submissive to those above us. In Titus Paul reveals that submission involves obedience. He reminds Christians "to be submissive to rulers and authorities, *to be obedient* . . . " (3:1). The parallel usages of submission and love elsewhere supports the contention that one cannot express his responsibility of love to higher governmental authorities without being obedient to their commands (cf. 1 Peter 3:1). Jesus said, "If you love me, you will keep my commandments" (John 14: 15).

Part of the obligation of one's Christian love, then, is expressed in obedience to his government. It is the Christian's duty to obey his government because God ordained government; to resist government is to resist the ordinance of God. Government was set up by God after the Flood (Gen. 9:6). Noah was given the sword to enforce it, and Paul recognized that government still had that sword (Rom. 13:4). Furthermore, Daniel recognized that the "Most High rules the kingdom of men, and gives it to whom he will, and sets over it the lowliest of men" (Dan. 4:17). Indeed, as Daniel experienced under Nebuchadnezzar and Paul under Nero, God sometimes sets up even the most wicked of men. The Christian, nonetheless, is obliged to respect the ruler for the sake of his office, "for he is God's servant for your sake . . . to execute his wrath on the wrongdoer" (Rom. 13:4, 5). Peter summed up the Christian's responsibility to obey government in these words, "Be subject for the Lord's sake to every human institution, whether it be to the emperor as supreme, or to governors as sent by him . . ." (1 Peter 2:13, 14).

Does this mean that one should obey his government in whatever it commands, even the command to go to war? This is the crucial question, and it does not have a simple answer. The reason one cannot give an unconditional "yes" answer is that the Bible indicates there are times when love demands disobedience to one's government. For instance, the three Hebrew men disobeyed the command of government to worship the great golden image of Nebuchadnezzar and were cast into the furnace (Dan. 3); Daniel refused to follow the king's edict to pray to no other God and was thrown into the den of lions (Dan. 6). In the New Testament, Peter and the apostles twice disobeyed the authorities who commanded them never to speak again in the name of Jesus (Acts 4, 5).

There are also examples which bear directly on the command of government to take lives. The Hebrew midwives were told to kill every male child born. They refused and the Bible says, "so God dealt well with the midwives . . . And because the midwives feared God he gave them families" (Exod. 1:20, 21). Obadiah was commanded by the wicked queen Jezebel to kill all the prophets. He refused and hid a hundred of them in a cave (1 Kings 18:4). These divinely approved cases of disobedience to government prove that a "My government, right or wrong" kind of obedience is definitely contrary to the principles of love. One is not obligated by the

obedience implied in love always to obey his
government's command to kill. War is not right
simply because a government has decreed it so.
Blind obedience to government to the point of
worshiping an idol is patriolatry. And unquestioning compliance with the command of an authority to kill may be just plain murder.

The obligation to government is only an obligation under God. In short, one should always obey
his government when it takes its place *under* God
but never when the government takes the place
of God. Clearly, only God has the right to command exclusive prayer and worship; also, no man
has a right to forbid a man not to give witness
to his faith in God or to kill innocent lives. And
when the government oversteps its subordination
to God, then its citizens are relieved of the responsibility to obey it. If one can escape an oppressive government, well and good; Moses and
the children of Israel escaped from Egypt (Exod.
12). If one cannot escape, then he must submit
to the consequences of his disobedience. The
apostles and early Christians were jailed, perse-
cuted and even martyred. Like the Old Testament saints before them, "some were tortured,
refusing to accept release (by denying their faith)
that they might rise again to a better life" (Heb.
11:35).

The love for God and for the innocent led
many believers to disobey the oppressive and
idolatrous commands of government. Love's obligation to obey higher human powers, even those
ordained of God, is not blind. One must always
be aware of the priority of love's demands i.e.,
the love of God over obedience to man and love

of the many over the wishes of the few, etc., (see Chapter 8). Christian love does not take the "easy" way out by hiding its individual responsibility in the collective responsibility of its government's command to kill. Love demands the "hard" choice of what is right for the individual in a specific war.

LOVE AND THE COMMAND OF JESUS NOT TO RESIST EVIL

The position that one ought *always* to obey his government to go to war is called activism. This, as we have just seen, is morally wrong. The view that one should *never* go to war is called pacifism. Is this morally right? Many Christians have interpreted the words of Jesus "not to resist evil" in this manner. Let us examine the pacifist's position.

Traditionally, biblical pacifism is built on two basic arguments. Another argument emerges from a more recent thought. (1) First, the Bible prohibits life-taking (Exod. 20:13). This moral command of God takes precedence over any human commands to go to war. The commands of conscience are more binding than the laws of state. The "commands" of God to kill in the Bible are concessional and/or conditional but not categorical and unconditional. They reflect at best God's permissive will but not His perfect will. There was a better way to treat one's enemies which Jesus brought to light in the New Testament, the way of love. This leads us to the second argument. (2) Forcefully and violently resisting evil is wrong. Jesus said, "Do not resist one who is evil. But if any one strikes you on the right cheek, turn to him the other also . . . and if any one forces you to go one mile, go with him two miles" (Matt. 6:39-41). Commenting on this passage, the apostle Paul adds, "repay no one evil for evil . . . so far as it depends on you, live peaceably with all . . . never avenge yourself. . . . Do not be overcome by evil, but overcome evil with good" (Rom. 12:17-21). The pacifist concludes from these passages that physical force, at least to the point of life-taking, is incompatible with the nature of Christian love.

(3) A third argument is a special extension of the second one. Participation in warfare is not essentially wrong for all men at all times but it is wrong for *all* Christians today. It is incongruous with God's special mission for His disciples in the Christian dispensation as the ambassadors of love and peace. How can Christians preach the peace of God while they are warring with men? How can they proclaim love while they are involved in the act of killing others? At least for the people of God in this age, war is incompatible with their calling as the children of love. In view of Christ's death and the announcement of the love ethic, war is divinely declared to be wrong as such. By a kind of progressive revelation God now pronounces wrong, in view of the cross of Christ and redeeming love, what before this divine expression of love was allowed or even commanded by God. War is wrong since the cross, even though God approved it before Christ. Like divorce, God permitted war because of the "hardness of men's hearts" but now in view of Christ God wishes to soften men's hearts by love.

The pacifist's view is believable and in many respects biblical, but it, too, is built on an "easy" and even "soft" view of love. Let us examine the arguments in the light of a biblical understanding of love. The first argument has been sufficiently answered in the preceding chapter. All life-taking is not wrong, only life-taking *as such* is always wrong. Or, more properly, life-taking is wrong but life-saving is not wrong. And sometimes it is necessary to sacrifice some lives to save others. The Bible provides many cases of justifiable life-taking or life-sacrificing: (1) Capital punishment (Gen. 9:6), (2) self-defense (Exod. 22:2), (3) sacrificial suicide (Samson, Christ), (4) rescuing the innocent (Gen. 14), (5) punishment of the wicked individuals (Num. 25:8), families (Joshua 7:25), and even whole nations (Joshua 10:40; cf. Lev. 18:24f.) 'are all instances of justifiable life-taking. Love can and often does demand the sacrifice of human lives. The innocent must be protected from the guilty and the many from the few.

The second argument of pacifism to the effect that Christians should not use force to resist evil is contrary to the teaching of the New Testament. (1) Jesus used physical force and a whip in cleansing the temple (John 2); (2) although Jesus forbade the use of the sword to defend or spread His kingdom (Matt. 26:52), He also commanded His disciples to buy a sword (apparently) for their own civil defense (Luke 22:36); (3) Jesus did not rebuke a soldier for his profession but only for unjust use of his power (Luke 3:14); (4) Paul demanded his rights as a citizen and accepted the protection of the Roman army when his life was threatened (Acts 22, 23); (5) Some early devout believers were soldiers (Acts 10:1);

(6) There is no evidence that Jesus intended nor that His disciples understood Him to take "resist not evil" any more universally or literally than "pluck out your eye." (There is no record that Jesus turned His cheek when smitten, John 19:3.)

The statements of Jesus in the Sermon on the Mount are intended to rebuke the retaliatory spirit of activism, not to forbid all efforts against evil. Nowhere does the Bible teach that love demands that we allow the innocent to be oppressed and killed without lifting a hand to help them. James said, "Whoever knows what is right to do and fails to do it, for him it is sin" (4:17). The kind of "love" which will do nothing for the cause of justice would be both empty-headed and hard-hearted. Love is not only for the enemy and the guilty; it is also for one's friends and the innocent. And when there is an aggressive action by the former on the latter, love demands strong and firm resistance. It is possible to love even one's enemies, and punish them at the same time. God loves and punishes His children (Heb. 12:5, 6) and so do good parents (Prov. 13:24). The love, in fact, is *in* the forceful action, not merely *alongside* of it. Resisting evil *is* an act of love, whether it is in members of one's own family or in other men.

The last argument of pacifism may be answered as follows: Love and life-saving are compatible in both Testaments. In fact, they are commanded in both. Jesus did not institute any new law of love; love is taught in both dispensations. Neither the character of God nor the commands built on it change from age to age (cf. Chapters 2 and 5). Jesus was not adding to the Law but fulfilling it

by bringing out and exemplifying its true teaching, as opposed to the misinterpretation of the
Law by some of the religious leaders of His day.
A case in point is the so-called imprecatory psalms.
Invoking God's judgment by prayer is not unique
to the Old Testament. Jesus commanded His
disciples to "shake off the dust of their feet"
(Mark 10:14) on the cities which receive not
the Gospel; Paul and Barnabas did exactly this
at Antioch (Acts 11:51). Even in heaven the
martyred saints utter an imprecation to God: "O
sovereign Lord, holy and true, how long before
thou wilt judge and avenge our blood on those
who dwell upon the earth?" (Rev. 6:10).

Furthermore, the Old Testament imprecations,
like the New, were not personal vendettas against
one's enemies. David, who wrote some of them,
was far from vindictive toward Saul; he could
have killed Saul on several occasions but refused
to do so even though Saul was in pursuit of David's life (cf. 1 Sam. 26). In fact, one of the imprecatory psalms flatly states that the author loved
his enemies: "in return for *my love* they accuse me,
even as *I make prayer for them.* So they reward
me evil for good and hatred for *my love*" (109:
4, 5). The imprecator was not grinding out his
personal grudges on his enemies; he was loving
and praying for them despite their misuse of him.
And because justice was not being accomplished,
the imprecator committed by prayer his just cause
to the righteous God to do the final judging.

There seems to be a confusion in the pacifist's
thinking between *taking vengeance* in one's own
hands and *defending the innocent* against evil
aggression. Vengeance does belong to the Lord

and engaging in wars out of vindictive motives is wrong. But justice is, in part, man's cause and the defense of the innocent is not wrong. It is in fact what love demands.

Radical activism is contrary to love because the obedience to higher human powers implied in total love is neither blind nor unconditional. And, pacifism is contrary to love because it forsakes the cause of the oppressed and innocent. It capitulates the total cause of justice to the after life. The Bible makes it unmistakably clear that Christians should be actively involved in promoting a just peace among men. Paul wrote, "If possible, so far as it depends upon you, live peaceably with all" (Rom. 12:18), and he urged prayer and effort be made "that we may lead a quiet and peaceable life, godly and respectful in every way" (1 Tim. 2:2). The prophets speak often about the one who "executes true justice between man and man" (Ezek. 18:8). Jesus called "justice" in this world one of the "weightier" matters of the law (Matt. 23:23). Total pacifism forsakes the very political process which alone can assure that justice. Total pacifism is, in fact, *political* "drop-outism." It cops out of the crucial political process (where the power is) in favor of *moral* influence and/or mere *social* action.

Love commits the Christian to working for justice in this world, and there is no way to assure justice in this world (of sinful men) without power, political power. This is why God instituted government after the violent predeluvian experience. Total pacifism confuses utopian or millennial expectations with the realities of a sinful world.

As a matter of fact, if we are interpreting correctly, even the millennial age of perfect justice will entail the need for strong political force to insure a just peace. For Christ will bring His reign with a "sharp sword" by which "he judges and makes war" (Rev. 19:11, 15); He will continue it for a "thousand years" ruling with a "rod of iron" (19:15; 20:4-7) at the end of which time another rebellion breaks out in which "the kings of the earth with their armies gather to make war against him . . ." (20:19). Man is a rebel, and the only way to insure peace and justice in this fallen world is with the kind of political power in which total pacifism, by its repudiation of force, cannot participate.

LOVE AND A JUST WAR

Love is left with but one alternative. It must weigh the alternatives implied in peace and justice and get involved. Total *activism* is blind, senseless obedience and complete *pacifism* is naive and unrealistic optimism. The former leads to patriolatry and murder; the latter leads to the oppression of the innocent and the triumph of injustice. Christian love demands *selectivism* on the question of war. Not every war is automatically just for a man simply because his country commands it. And, hear this, not every war is wrong simply because his conscience forbids it. Conscience can be wrong; it can be conditioned by culture, sentiment, and expedience (cf. Rom. 2:15; 1 Tim. 4:2). To correct this, conscience should be informed by the realities of life and the responsibility of love. The latter compels one to get involved in the political process for justice and peace.

If Christian love leads to selectivism in warfare, it is important to determine precisely what would constitute a just war. For if not all wars are just, then one must ask which ones are and which are not, in order that he may fulfill his responsibility of love. The answer to this question is implicit in the principles of love discussed in Chapter 8. Especially pertinent are the following: (1) Persons are more valuable than things; (2) Persons who respect personhood are to be preferred over those who do not; (3) Many lives are of more value than few lives. Either implied or stated in these principles is the justification of a just war, viz., it would be a war to save many lives at the sacrifice of a few; it would be a war against those who disrespect persons in defense of those being disrespected; it would be a war defending the value of persons over the value of things, i.e., against those who put economic or territorial gain above the value of human lives.

When the implications of these principles are spelled out in terms of the modern situation with the aid of biblical principles and illustrations, something like the following minimal components of a just war emerge. A just war is one which is:

(1) *Declared and engaged in by proper authority.* Since God instituted government, men are not to take justice in their individual hands. God gave the sword to government (Gen. 9:6) and it is government alone which has the right to wage war against other governments, not individuals (cf. Rom. 13:4). The individual, of course, has the right to protect himself against other individuals (Exod. 22:2), but he has no

right to fight against his government. He must either escape, if it is oppressive, or submit (Exod. 12; 1 Peter 2:13);

(2) *Engaged in for the protection of the innocent.* Wars of aggression are not engaged in out of love. A just war is fought in defense of the oppressed and innocent, just as Abraham rescued Lot from the kings of the valley who had unjustly captured him (Gen. 14:14f.). (The size of Abraham's army, God's call upon him to become a great "nation," and the fact that he waged a successful war against several other kingdoms clearly indicate that he was not acting as an individual but as a proper governmental authority.) Another example of the principle of protecting the innocent is the appeal of Paul to Rome and the acceptance of military protection from evil men who sought his life (Acts 22, 23);

(3) *Fought only if all peaceful negotiations fail to attain justice.* The Christian must always, "*if possible,* so far as it depends on him, live peaceably with all." Jesus said, "blessed are the peacemakers." The children of Israel were commanded, "when you draw near to a city to fight against it, offer terms of peace to it . . . But if it makes no peace with you, but makes war against you, then you shall beseige it" (Deut. 20:10). Of course, if a country finds itself being attacked, then "negotiations" failed (maybe there were none) and they must defend themselves. But every effort should be made to "strive for peace with all men . . . " (Heb. 12:14);

(4) *Fought with the realistic expectation of success.* A war which has no hope of being suc-

cessful amounts to no more than a protest which sacrifices *more* innocent lives to the guilty than no war would have done. A just war must have calculated odds for success or it will amount to a merciless slaughter of the innocent. The principle of just warfare is to protect the innocent, not sacrifice them unnecessarily and unsuccessfully. Mass suicide is morally wrong;

(5) *A justly waged war.* Finally, a just war must be justly waged. A just cause could be fought but should not be fought in an unjust way. Two wrongs do not constitute a right. God's people in the Old Testament were told, "when you beseige a city for a long time, making war against it in order to take it, you shall not destroy the trees by wielding an ax against them. . . . Only the trees which you know are not trees for food you may destroy and cut down that you may build siegeworks against the city that makes war with you until it falls" (Deut. 20:19, 20). The principle here is to avoid unnecessary destruction, especially that which is necessary to the continuation of life after the war. The same principle would apply to lives during the war. Non-military personnel should not be military targets. In specific terms, even granting that the Viet Nam war was just, My Lai was unjust.

Now in view of these biblical principles of just warfare there are certain conclusions which may be applied to our contemporary situation. First, all-out nuclear war (or whatever would initiate it) is certainly contrary to love. It would involve too great a sacrifice of innocent human lives. The price would not be worth the cause whatever the alleged injustice. Most men would prefer living with injustice (with the hope for change) than not living at all. This means that macro-nuclear wars are always unjust wars. In brief, Christian love demands macro-nuclear pacifism. The view that declares that if there are only two people surviving a global nuclear war, then they should be from "my" country is immoral. (The use of micro-nuclear devices in limited warfare is not necessarily unethical, but civilians should not be the target.)

Second, granting the justice of the Second World War and granting that the demonstration of nuclear power would save the thousands of lives lost in invading Japan to consummate the war, it seems wrong that the bomb was dropped on people. A warning and demonstration of the power on a vacant island would no doubt have accomplished the same without the terrible loss of human life.

Third, Christian love demands that we work for realistic bilateral disarmament, especially of nuclear weapons. Love says, "Let not the H-bomb be the sequel in which all men are cremated equal."

As we have said, the Christian ethic is not a clear-cut set of rules which demand no struggle and decision by the believer. On the contrary, the Christian ethic of love demands the deepest involvement. There is the need to immerse one's self in the Scriptures to know God, His laws and the exemplary life of His Son. Jesus often charged the religious people of His day saying, "You are wrong because you know neither the scriptures nor the power of God" (Matt. 22:29). Further, the Christian must be involved directly in weighing the alternatives to determine which course

of action will really be most in accord with the
scriptural commands. Finally, the Christian must
act on his ethic. Merely knowing the path of
love is not sufficient; the Christian must *take* that
path in a world of indifference and hate. Indeed,
the Christian love ethic by its very nature calls
for deep and personal involvement; for it is of
the essence of Christ's love to be deeply and personally involved with human needs.